Praise for Peter School Climate

Peter DeWitt has provided us with a powerful and timely book on the growing phenomenon of collective efficacy. The six chapters contain a gold mine of ideas, resources, tools, surveys, action steps, and reflective questions. What I like best is that the book is grounded equally in research and practice. This is an urgently needed book, and you will learn a lot from it!

—**Michael Fullan,** Professor Emeritus
OISE/University of Toronto
Ontario, Canada

While schools focus on common standards, data analysis, and increasing achievement, Peter DeWitt explains the critical nature of school climate and why, as the "5th C," it is imperative for school success. As a school leader, DeWitt often asked thought-provoking questions, engaged in challenging conversations, and encouraged reflection, much as he does in *School Climate: Leading With Collective Efficacy.* Through interesting vignettes, personal experience, and a variety of research, DeWitt provides a practical approach for growing a rich, safe environment.

—**Melissa J. Weatherwax,** MSEd
Former Classroom Teacher
K–12 Instructional Technology Specialist
Averill Park, NY

If you are a fan of cooperative learning like I am and believe in the power of teamwork, this book is for you. Whether you are a district leader, school principal, or classroom teacher, you will find useful the numerous examples and practical ideas that Peter DeWitt offers in this book. *School Climate: Leading With Collective Efficacy* shows how one plus one can sometimes be three in collectively led schools.

—**Pasi Sahlberg,** Author
Finnish Lessons 2.0
Helsinki, Finland

DeWitt's book provides hands-on information on how collaborative leadership can help you create a school climate with the focus on learning—one in which all students (and teachers) feel they belong and are able to grow. Each chapter ends with action steps and questions to help me find the confidence to lead my team towards collective efficacy, including my own, without avoiding the tough topics.

—**Claire Ohlenschlager,** MEd, English Department Chair
School of Education—Rotterdam University
of Applied Sciences
Rotterdam, The Netherlands

(Continued)

This is a fabulous book by a renowned expert in the field of leadership. Peter DeWitt explains the complex and credible in a way that is thought-provoking, challenging, and inspiring. I love how he gives insights in what successful collaborative leadership is and shows how we can all build our skills and mindset for leading towards collective efficacy.

—**James Nottingham,** Author, *Challenging Learning*
Creator of #TheLearningPit
JN Partnership LTD
Northumberland, United Kingdom

In *School Climate: Leading With Collective Efficacy,* Peter DeWitt delivers in print what he so readily delivers in person—clarity and coherence around a most important topic. As a former high school principal and district leader, DeWitt leaves me with both the confidence that I can do this and the understanding of how I can make progress, starting today. This is a must read for any school leader.

—**Kerry Alcorn,** Teacher/Author/Leader
Saskatoon Public School Division
Saskatoon, Canada

Peter DeWitt gives school leaders exactly what they need—research-based school improvement strategies that work effectively in schools today. Our instructional leadership teams that worked with DeWitt over the past year to build teachers' self-efficacy and collective teacher efficacy are now coconstructing a school culture in which everyone not only grows, but thrives. *School Climate: Leading With Collective Efficacy* is a road map to this proven approach to student success.

—**Matthew Bolduc,** Director of Curriculum
and Professional Development
Bellingham Public Schools
Bellingham, MA

Supported by current educational research and grounded in powerful leadership narratives, DeWitt offers a compelling case for leaders and learning communities to collaborate to achieve collective efficacy for student success. The practical strategies, research citations, conceptual frameworks, rubrics, and self-assessment tools provide leaders with practical instruments for reflection, setting intentions, securing accountability, and measuring the impact of a collaborative climate and culture.

—**Jill Ott,** Project Lead—Supporting LGBTQ Students
Ontario Principals' Council
Ontario, Canada

As educators, we consistently hear about the importance of collaboration, critical thinking, communication, and creatively, and in *School Climate,* Peter DeWitt highlights the additional key element—climate. By providing action steps, discussion questions, and reflective tools, this book helps guide teachers, leaders, and those teachers who aspire to be leaders to develop a positive school climate. Increased self-awareness encourages teachers to become more reflective and effective, which develops a more collaborative school climate. Providing effective strategies throughout, this book is relevant and applicable to all school contexts, teams, and individuals.

—**Andrea Stringer,** Professional Learning Coach
Sydney, Australia

After reading DeWitt's book on collaborative leadership and school climate, my own self-efficacy improved. I closed its cover feeling empowered and eager to share what I'd learned. The discussion questions bring practicality to the possibility of implementation and excitement about the potential results.

—**Sera Deo,** MST, Fourth-Grade Teacher
Miller Hill Elementary School
Averill Park, NY

Where am I going? How am I going? Where to next? These are all simple yet aspirational questions we ask our students to answer daily, but are we ready to ask this of ourselves in relation to our leadership of school climate and collective efficacy? Peter DeWitt is comprehensive yet succinct, producing a practical guide for developing individual and collective efficacy in an inclusive, positive school climate. Research-based strategies, thought-provoking questions, and effective tools are at your fingertips, ready for immediate use. If you're after a good read, that's exactly what you'll get here . . . but if you're after an essential resource to empower your school community through the strength of belief that they can make learning happen, you will get that and more.

—**Ben Walsh,** Principal
Picnic Point Public School
Sydney, NSW, Australia

School Climate: Leading With Collective Efficacy is an impressive follow-up to DeWitt's previous book, *Collaborative Leadership: Six Influences That Matter Most.* In his latest offering, DeWitt offers practical yet deep advice and strategies for improving school climate for the benefit of students, families, teachers, and administrators. Throughout the book, he communicates by seamlessly combining research with his experiences and the accounts of other professionals in the field. Many ideas can be implemented tomorrow, and DeWitt's main points are those with which any educational leader could identify. If you are looking for a book to assist you on your journey to advancing your leadership abilities, your school, or your district, look no further!

—**Ross Cooper,** Supervisor of Instructional Practice K–12
Coauthor of *Hacking Project Based Learning*
Apple Distinguished Educator

School Climate: Leading With Collective Efficacy combines the research, anecdotes, reflection questions, and action steps necessary to become a high-impact, capacity-building school leader. DeWitt's style—all-at-once relatable and grounded in the work of John Hattie and so many others—will prompt readers to consider the essential aspects to our work together to be catalysts for progress in teacher and community learning, as well as in student achievement.

—**Dennis J. Schug Jr.,** Principal
Hampton Bays Middle School
Hampton Bays, NY

To Mom, Doug, and Trish. Without you,
I would not be in this position.
Thank you for all of your support.

School Climate

Leading With Collective Efficacy

Peter M. DeWitt

A Joint Publication

FOR INFORMATION:

Corwin

A SAGE Company

2455 Teller Road

Thousand Oaks, California 91320

(800) 233-9936

www.corwin.com

SAGE Publications Ltd.

1 Oliver's Yard

55 City Road

London EC1Y 1SP

United Kingdom

SAGE Publications India Pvt. Ltd.

B 1/I 1 Mohan Cooperative Industrial Area

Mathura Road, New Delhi 110 044

India

SAGE Publications Asia-Pacific Pte. Ltd.

3 Church Street

#10-04 Samsung Hub

Singapore 049483

Executive Editor: Arnis Burvikovs

Senior Associate Editor: Desirée A. Bartlett

Editorial Assistant: Kaitlyn Irwin

Production Editor: Melanie Birdsall

Copy Editor: Amy Hanquist Harris

Typesetter: C&M Digitals (P) Ltd.

Proofreader: Ellen Brink

Indexer: Diggs Publication Services

Cover Designer: Michael Dubowe

Marketing Manager: Nicole Franks

Chapter-opening image courtesy of ©iStockphoto.com/rdonar

Chapter 3 flag icon courtesy of ©iStockphoto.com/RamCreativ

Printed in the United States of America

Library of Congress Cataloging-in-Publication Data

Names: DeWitt, Peter M., author.

Title: School climate : leading with collective efficacy / Peter M. DeWitt.

Description: First edition. | Thousand Oaks, California : Corwin, 2018. | Includes bibliographical references and index.

Identifiers: LCCN 2017011445 | ISBN 9781506385990 (pbk. : alk. paper)

Subjects: LCSH: School environment. | Classroom environment. | Educational leadership.

Classification: LCC LC210 .D495 2018 | DDC 371.102/4—dc23

LC record available at https://lccn.loc.gov/2017011445

This book is printed on acid-free paper.

Certified Chain of Custody
Promoting Sustainable Forestry
www.sfiprogram.org
SFI-01268

SUSTAINABLE FORESTRY INITIATIVE

SFI label applies to text stock

18 19 20 21 10 9 8 7 6 5 4 3 2

Contents

Preface

Teachers and leaders know how important school climate is, but they're not always sure they have the time necessary to focus on it. With *School Climate: Leading With Collective Efficacy*, it is my goal to provide K–12 school leaders, prospective school leaders, teachers, and coaches practical, high-impact strategies that will help improve their school climate, deepen their involvement in learning with students, and help them engage more parents.

In this book, you will find

- **Stories:** Readers will find school stories from practitioners around North America, Australia, and the United Kingdom. Each story focuses on school climate and authentic engagement of the different stakeholders who make up the school community.
- **Trudy and Tim:** Throughout the book, you will hear about the experiences of Dr. Trudy Cowen, an elementary school principal, and Tim Cooper, a high school principal. Including stories from Trudy and Tim as a running thread throughout the book will help readers see two very different approaches to school climate and their varied results.
- **Evidence to support the suggested strategies:** This book focuses on the important self-efficacy work of Albert Bandura and the collective efficacy work of Megan Tschannen-Moran and Marilyn Barr.

- **Tools:** There will be frameworks throughout the book that will revolve around the teacher observation cycle.
- **Early Warning System (EWS):** One of the best features about this book is the guidance it offers for creating an EWS at your school. The EWS described in this book comprises a list of indicators to identify students before they become at risk, as well as a set of possible interventions to ensure that they do not in fact become at risk.
- **Action steps:** Each chapter ends with a list of suggested action steps that you can take to improve school climate in your own setting.
- **Discussion questions:** Each chapter ends with a set of discussion questions you can work on with your school leadership team to improve school climate together.

It is always my hope to find a balance between offering practices that readers can use tomorrow and the research to support the need to do it. I believe I have done that in this book. As a former principal, there is nothing more important to me than a focus on school climate. In order to maximize the learning that takes place in school, we all need a supportive and inclusive school climate in which we can take risks as professionals to improve the lives of the students we serve. It is my hope that as you read this book you will find new ideas in each chapter to incorporate into your everyday practices and that by the end of this book you will have transformed the school climate that you work so hard to lead.

Acknowledgments

When writing acknowledgments, it's impossible to thank everyone. I feel very fortunate to do the work I do because I have had the opportunity to work with some people I have long admired and met others on the road whom I have learned a lot from in our conversations and interactions.

There are a few people, however, that I want to thank because their help led me to writing this book:

- Frank, Jody, Pam, Hassan, Dawn, Edd, and my nephews and nieces . . . the great ones too!
- John Hattie, Jim Knight, Russ Quaglia, Michael Fullan, Andy Hargreaves, and Jenni Donohoo. Thank you for the friendship, feedback, and mentoring. Your work inspires me every day.
- My Corwin family. Too many to count. Thanks for all of the opportunities, support, and the camaraderie.
- Tim Dawkins, Lisa Meade, Patti Siano, Vicky Day, Christina Luce, Jill Berkowicz, Ross Cooper, and Michelle Hebert.
- Arnis Burvikovs, Desirée Bartlett, Ariel Bartlett, and Kaitlyn Irwin. Your editing and feedback make me a better writer.
- Alejandro Rivera, Alina Davis, Andrew Greene, Billy Krakower, Donald Gately, Ellen O'Neill, Dennis Schug, Erin Marone, Fred Ende, John Christie, and Ned Dale. Thank you for inviting me to be a part of the Collaborative Leadership Voxer Group.

Publisher's Acknowledgments

Corwin gratefully acknowledges the contributions of the following reviewers:

Virginia E. Kelsen, PhD, Executive Director, Career Readiness
Chaffey Joint Union High School District
Ontario, Canada

Louis Lim, Vice-Principal
Bayview Secondary School, York
Richmond Hill, Ontario, Canada

Lynn Macan, Visiting Assistant Professor
University at Albany–SUNY
Albany, NY

Jordan Nelson, Principal
Maxwell CSD
Carlisle, IA

LaQuita Outlaw, Principal, Grades 6–8
Bay Shore Middle School
Bay Shore, NY

Karen L. Tichy, Assistant Professor of Educational Leadership
Saint Louis University
St. Louis, MO

Patricia L. Tucker, Regional Superintendent, Retired
District of Columbia Public Schools
Washington, DC

David Stegall, Superintendent
Newton-Conover City Schools
Newton, NC

Janice Wyatt-Ross, Director
Fayette County Public Schools
Lexington, KY

About the Author

Peter M. DeWitt (EdD) taught for 11 years and was a school principal for eight years. He runs workshops and provides keynotes that focus on collaborative leadership, the fostering of inclusive school climates, and connected learning.

Peter is a Visible Learning Trainer for John Hattie, Instructional Coach for Jim Knight, and Student Voice Advocate for Russ Quaglia, working nationally and internationally. He is the series editor for the *Connected Educator* Series (Corwin) and the *Impact Leadership* Series (Corwin).

His *Finding Common Ground* blog is published by *Education Week*, and he is a freelance writer for *Vanguard* magazine (SAANYS). He is the 2013 School Administrators Association of New York State's (SAANYS) Outstanding Educator of the Year and the 2015 Bammy Award winner for Education Blogger of the Year (Academy of Education Arts and Sciences).

Peter's first educational book, *Dignity for All: Safeguarding LGBT Students*, was published in 2012 and was the topic of his doctoral dissertation. In 2013, Peter contributed a chapter to *De-Testing and De-Grading Schools: Authentic Alternatives to*

Accountability and Standardization (Peter Lang, 2013). His other books include *School Climate Change: How Do I Foster a Positive School Climate* (ASCD, 2014; coauthored with Sean Slade) and *Flipping Leadership Doesn't Mean Reinventing the Wheel* (Corwin, 2014). Peter is the cochair of the National School Climate Council. His articles have appeared in education journals at the state, national, and international level. He has written for *Principal Magazine, Education Week, Educational Leadership, The Huffington Post,* PBS, ASCD Whole Child, *Connected Principals, SmartBlogs,* and *ASCD Express.*

Peter has presented at forums, conferences, and panel discussions at state, national, and international conferences. Some of the highlights have been to present for the National Association of Elementary School Principals (NAESP, 2012, 2014, 2015), the Association of Supervision and Curriculum Development (ASCD, 2012, 2015, 2016), ICLE's Model Schools, and Osiris World Conference in London and to sit on a school safety panel on NBC's *Education Nation* with Goldie Hawn and Hoda Kotb.

Peter has worked with the American Association of School Administrators (AASA), the National Education Association (NEA), the National Association of Secondary School Principals (NASSP), the National Association of School Psychologists, the Association of Supervision and Curriculum Development (ASCD), the National School Climate Center, GLSEN, PBS, NBC, NPR, BAM Radio Network, and ABCNews.com.

Introduction

A Tale of Two Leaders

Meet Tim

Tim Cooper is the principal of Waterville High School. Although he has 2,000 students in his high school, he and his two assistant principals work hard to make the rounds and engage with students. He stands in the parking lot when students drive in so he can tell them to have a good day, and he's also there when they leave, when he tells them to "be safe." We know how new drivers can be.

Whether it's students getting off the bus, being dropped off by their relatives, or driving their own cars, Mr. Cooper and his two assistant principals spread the wealth when it comes to building relationships with students. They understand that not all students come from the more supportive households or situations, so they do their best to show they care with one-minute conversations at a time.

When adult visitors walk into the school, they feel welcome. Families often remark how Waterville High School doesn't seem like the high school they attended because it feels very student-centered and warm. There is student art-work on the walls, which as we know from art class, can be very haunting, alluring, and sometimes humorous because of the various interpretations by students. Tim likes that because he believes it reflects the diversity of his student population, whether it be by race, gender, sexual orientation, or religion.

And then there is Mrs. Choukeir, the main office admin-istrative assistant who sits in the front office welcoming students, answering the phone, and checking in guests. She tries her best to remember the names of parents, and she definitely knows the names of the students. After being at the school for 10 years, she knows the stories of the students because she lives in town, has seen their older siblings go through the school, and even graduated with some of their parents. Although this is a high school and the students aren't always the kindest and the most awake in the morning, the team in the main office does its best to get the students' day off to the best start.

When it comes to formal pieces of school life, Tim does his best to collaborate with his staff. He coconstructs formal observations with each teacher and asks his assistant princi-pals to do the same. Teachers each choose a goal, and then Tim sends them an article, YouTube video, Khan Academy video, or blog to help them see what the goal done successfully will look like. When he conducts the observation, he walks around with his iPad, writing notes as he quietly talks with students to ask what they are learning at the same time he watches the delivery of the teacher. Luckily, because of the amount of time Tim spends in classrooms the students do not think twice that he is in there. Due to it being a high school with a large popula-tion, Tim isn't able to get into classrooms every day; however, between his time in the parking lot and in the hallways as well as the classrooms, Tim is a recognized and welcomed figure when he walks into the classrooms.

Delivering feedback after a formal observation is a differ-ent experience in Waterville High School as well. Tim provides teachers with all of his iPad notes well before they meet in person. The formal observation meeting, as much as possible, happens in the teacher's classroom and not in the main office because Tim likes to go to the teacher's comfort zone, where he focuses on her or his strengths more and deficits less. He even goes back through the classroom when time allows to see if the teacher is still working toward his or her goal. If he can't get to the classroom, Tim does find time to ask the teacher how the goal is going. It's something that educators have come to expect at Waterville High School.

Additionally, Tim's faculty meetings are not seen as traditional faculty meetings as much as they are seen as professional development sessions. There is a group of teachers, as well as each department chair, that sits on the instructional leadership team (ILT). Two teachers act as chairpersons, and together as a group, they define the school climate goal that aligns with the district goal of "Every student will learn to his or her potential." Together, they create a learning goal for each faculty meeting and use the World Café model to run the faculty meeting as a workshop. No, not all teachers are on board, but more and more are getting committed because they can clearly see that the goal of the faculty meeting is based on a conversation they may have had with their department chair.

When it comes to students at risk, Tim and his team developed an Early Warning System for their school, and the EWS team includes the nurse, school psychologist, social worker, and several teachers as well as special-area teachers. The EWS team looks over data that teachers have submitted about students they feel are most at risk. What makes the data different is not that it focuses on standardized tests, but that it includes a student engagement piece and a section in which teachers explain how they are using different strategies to engage their students. The EWS team focuses on academic as well as the social-emotional learning of students.

Perhaps it is due to Tim's own self-efficacy that he is a collaborative leader, or maybe it is to the credit of his former principal who helped guide him, but Waterville High School is an inclusive and supportive school climate. Visitors can see that when they see students deliver the news or they see the multiple diversity groups that take place afters school at the same time the sports teams practice. The artwork and Makerspace projects that line the halls and sit in display cases, the diversity of books and novels offered in the library, and the curriculum that focuses on social-emotional learning as much as innovative academic curriculum all contribute to the positive school climate.

Meet Trudy

Across the Waterville School District is a very different story . . .

Dr. Trudy Cowen had been a math coordinator for the school for seven years before taking the principalship at Eagle Elementary School. She took over the position from Mike Naylor, who had been the principal for 25 years. When Trudy took over the position, people in the school were ready for change. They were excited for what was to come because most teachers had not had great experiences with Mike. He was known to battle with the union over petty issues, which exploded into rigidity on both sides. He held faculty meetings that lasted 30 minutes but required staff to stay in the meeting for a full hour because they were contractually obligated to do so.

Trudy was a welcomed change from the constant battles for some of the staff. Others, not so much—they liked Mike and found him easy to get along with because he left them alone in the classroom. He stopped in to see them only when he needed to discipline a student or complete a teacher observation, which didn't always result in any new learning, but most of the teachers received *Exceeded Expectations* ratings on their evaluations, so his hands-off style worked for them.

Early on in her leadership at Eagle, Trudy ran a tight ship. Unlike Tim, Trudy did not have great experiences with her former school leaders, and her self-efficacy was never quite as high as it could have been before she received the position from the Waterville District Board of Education. Every day, Trudy would drive to work, worrying that she didn't know everything that was happening in her school. What if a parent knocked on her door and Trudy couldn't answer what was happening in the child's classroom? What if she couldn't get the test scores to be as high as her predecessor? What would happen if the board of education didn't think she was as strong as she came off in the interview?

Trudy worked hard at changing some of the flexibility that had happened, in her opinion, for way too long. She wanted everyone to know she was the opposite of Mike Naylor. Although Trudy was in the main office every morning when teachers arrived to sign into the building, she would not smile and would make them go to her office if she "had something to talk about" with them, which was code for "reprimand." Trudy would often be heard talking at students walking in the hallway, wondering where they were going or telling them to hurry up when they stepped off the bus or out of the car of the relative dropping them off. If they couldn't produce a hall pass during the day when requested, they—and their teacher—would be reprimanded by Trudy. Quite honestly, even teachers walking down the hallway during their prep time would be asked where they were going and why they weren't in their classes.

To make matters worse, there were times teachers walked down the hallway alone toward Trudy and said good morning to her, and she didn't respond at all. The next day, the same teacher would once again be in the same position, and Trudy would smile and say hello. From one day to the next, the hallway experience would be different. And speaking of the hallway, student artwork was not allowed to hang because Trudy was always prepared for the fire inspection. Although the fire inspection always allowed a certain percentage of work to hang on the walls, Trudy preferred that there wasn't a lot there. She actually preferred to keep the posters hanging on the wall that focused on behavior or students trying their best on tests.

The whole staff received e-mails from Trudy that stated teachers needed to be on time to the lunchroom to pick up their students, even though it was only a handful of teachers who were ever actually late. And during private, closed-door conversations, Trudy would get up and walk out several times midsentence, or she might share in confidence which teachers were failing at their jobs.

Teachers had to hand in lesson plan books every three weeks, something that they had never had to do before. Faculty meetings were shorter, which was a good thing, but Trudy stood at the front of the library and talked through a list of tasks that she expected each teacher to complete. There was not a lot of dialogue.

The lack of dialogue showed up during teacher observations as well. Trudy knew the previous principal was good at giving out *Exceeding Expectations* ratings, and she was not going to follow down the same path—in fact, she believed only about 10 percent of the teachers should get that rating. When she walked into a classroom with her iPad, she sat in the back of the room and watched every move of the teacher and then would type everything into her notes. Those notes stayed with her, and she used them as discussion points during the formal conversation at the end of the evaluation. Unfortunately, the teachers didn't get a lot of insight into what she was looking for when they met during the preobservation meetings because Trudy would spend that time asking questions about student misbehavior and what students were at risk of not meeting the standard on the state assessment in the spring.

That concern for test scores bled into recess as well. Trudy reduced the amount of recess for all students. Students could go outside only three times a week because they needed extended learning time the other two days in order to raise their test scores from the previous year. People soon found out that if they didn't agree with Trudy's methods, their class list and grade level they taught would look very different the next year.

There was even a time when a teacher handed his lesson plans in a day late because he forgot (even though he always had them done), and when he apologized as he handed the lesson plans to Trudy, she responded that it didn't matter because she never checked his plans anyway—and then she handed them back and walked into her office, shutting the door behind her. The teacher realized that after months of handing in his lesson plans on command, his principal never really looked at what was in them, even though they had a red mark on the page of the week she was checking.

Leadership and School Climate

If you don't think school climate and leadership matter, you haven't worked at a school where you weren't sure what your leader would say to you from one day to the next. Don't get me wrong, I have been fortunate to work for some great leaders, but one year under bad leadership, whether it comes from insecurity or unpreparedness, can destroy the self-efficacy of some of the most positive teachers. Other times, teachers find their leaders within because they know that schools, students, and teachers deserve better than they are getting.

It is not my intent to pick on Trudy and highlight Tim as I go through this book, but they have very different styles, and both stories are based on real situations. Yes, the names have been changed to protect the innocent and not so innocent, but they are the stories of two types of leaders we have running schools and contributing, either positively or negatively, to school climate daily. You will see their names appear throughout the text, and at the end of each chapter, I ask you to put yourself in their place and answer what they would do in given situations.

Leadership is important. Throughout the following chapters, it is my hope that you engage in dialogue about ideas that are shared that will help you focus on being more collaborative so that your school climate can be as positive and engaging as

Tim Cooper's and less like Trudy Cowen's. As you ponder the idea of leadership and school climate, here are some questions for you to reflect upon:

- Why does collaborative leadership interest you?
- What does school climate really mean to you?
- Are you conscious of whether your actions and the climate of the school you lead empowers or enables teachers and students?
- How will you inspire others to increase their own self-efficacy and build collective efficacy among staff?
- What evidence will you collect to understand your current reality?
- Whom do you identify with most—Trudy or Tim?

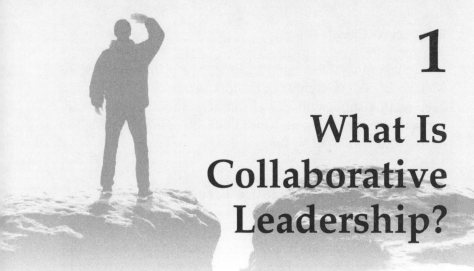

1

What Is Collaborative Leadership?

*Whatever one's style, every leader, to be effective, must have
and work on improving his or her moral purpose.*

—Michael Fullan

I n our leadership training, we are told to be visible. After all,
it's important to be seen in the hallway, on the sidewalk,
and in the cafeteria. Being visible contributes to a safe school
climate, partly because visibility means that leaders are present and able to maintain a calm atmosphere. Behavior changes
when the principal is around, right? However, what we
learned from Dr. Trudy Cowen's leadership is that we can be
visible but contribute to a negative school climate at the same
time. It's more important to engage positively with teachers,
families, and students. We, as leaders, need to create positive
relationships with the different stakeholders in the school
community, as Tim Cooper does at Waterville High School,
because that all leads to a more positive and engaging school
climate. Tim exemplifies the idea of collaborative leadership.

Collaborative leadership includes the purposeful actions we take as leaders to enhance the instruction of teachers, build deep relationships with all stakeholders through understanding self-efficacy (0.63), and build collective efficacy (1.57) to deepen our learning together.

The Hattie Effect

You will notice that there are numbers next to self-efficacy and collective efficacy, which will play an important part in this book. Those numbers, referred to as *effect sizes*, come from the work of John Hattie (2009, 2012a). Hattie's research, which provides the best lens on what works in education, involves over 1,500 meta-analyses and 300 million students. Hattie's research focuses on influences on learning. For example, some of the influences that have an important impact on learning are feedback (0.75), classroom discussion (0.80), and reciprocal teaching (0.74). All of the influences Hattie has researched come with effect sizes.

If the influence has an effect size of 0.40, which Hattie refers to as *the hinge point*, it equates to a year's worth of growth for a year's input. Any influence with an effect greater than 0.40 equates to more than a year's worth of growth, and any influence with an effect size lower than 0.40 equates to less than a year's worth of growth for a year's input. For example, in the definition of *self-efficacy*, which refers to the belief we have in ourselves that we can make learning happen or can have an impact on the learning of our students, you saw that it had an effect size of 0.63. Additionally, collective teacher efficacy has an effect size of 1.57, which equates to almost four years of growth on the part of the teacher. On the other side of the scale, retention has an effect size of –0.13, which has a negative impact on learning.

Hattie's research revolves around a list of influences on learning, or strategies or circumstances that have an impact on learning, such as classroom discussion, reciprocal teaching, metacognitive activities, student mobility, and family engagement. The list of influences grew from 138 in 2009 to 150 in 2015 and far beyond 250 today (Hattie, 2015a, 2016). His research has been used by ministries of education, countless teachers and leaders, and has professionally been implemented in over 7,000 schools.

Hattie's work is not without some criticism. School and district leaders need to be careful to understand the nuances of the research's implications before making policy decisions based on the work. One such criticism states that when the meta-analysis is averaged with the effect size of the research, the researcher misses out on certain nuances in the research (Killian, 2015). For example, school leadership has an effect size of 0.39, but when you take out the moderators of transformational leadership versus instructional leadership, you will find that transformational leadership has an effect size of 0.11, while instructional leadership's effect size is 0.41.

People who read Hattie's more recent work (2015c)—and are not aware that the influences are an average—tend to jump to different conclusions than those who understand the averaging because they look at the effect size as the be-all and end-all, and it is not. There is much more to the story. School leaders need to keep in mind the specific culture and students in their schools whenever they aggregate this kind of data. To get the deeper story, educators must read Hattie's original work (2009) on specific influences. Despite the criticism, I have included Hattie's research here because it offers us important insight into learning and provides the catalyst we need to kick off these important conversations.

The Importance of Self-Efficacy

Secondly, let's take time to understand self-efficacy and collective efficacy because they are central themes in the book. Bandura (1994) defines *self-efficacy* as "people's beliefs about their capabilities to produce designated levels of performance that exercise influence over events that affect their lives. Self-efficacy beliefs determine how people feel, think, motivate themselves and behave" (p. 2).

This concept of self-efficacy was first introduced by Bandura (1977) and focused on whether individuals believed that they had the capabilities to meet the demands of a specific task. McCormick, Tangum, and López-Forment (2002) suggest that "research findings have demonstrated a consistent relationship between self-efficacy and work-related performance" (p. 35). That work-related performance can contribute to a more productive and innovative school climate.

Building Self-Efficacy

We build self-efficacy in these ways:

- Providing support to teachers through supplying resources they need (e.g., articles, sacred prep time, and professional development based on their needs)
- Coconstructing goals with them
- Giving feedback around those goals

Through collaborative leadership, teachers with a low level of self-efficacy can change their mindsets to have a strong sense of one. In fact, McCormick and colleagues (2002) suggest that "efficacy beliefs are derived from experience" (p. 38), and collaborative leaders help contribute to efficacy through providing positive experiences to teachers, students, and parents. Bandura (1986) has identified four major categories of experiences that influence efficacy. A discussion of those four categories follows.

Experiences That Influence Efficacy

Personal performance accomplishments: A challenging activity brings out the strongest indicators for changing self-efficacy.

Vicarious experiences: McCormick et al. (2002) write, "By observing new skills and strategies in others, people enhance their task capabilities" (p. 38).

Positive feedback: In Bandura's research he referred to this as *social persuasion*. However, feedback was one of the major contributors. Positive feedback, when given correctly, helps to increase a person's level of self-efficacy.

Physiological condition: Social and emotional well-being matter because they contribute to a person's level of self-efficacy. (Bandura, 1986)

All four categories have a strong relationship to leadership, and throughout the book, self-efficacy will be explored through the lens of students, teachers, families, and leaders. Collaboration is an important element of those four categories, and examples that fit into these four categories will be provided throughout the book.

Thirdly, in the collaborative leadership definition the topic of collective teacher efficacy was used. Tschannen-Moran and Barr (2004) define *collective teacher efficacy* as "the collective self-perception that teachers in a given school make an educational difference to their students over and above the educational impact of their homes and communities" (p. 190). The collective efficacy of teachers leads to a stronger school climate for students.

Building Collective Teacher Efficacy

We build collective teacher efficacy in these ways:

- Collaborative inquiry (Donohoo, 2016)
- Authentic professional learning communities (PLCs), in which teachers engage in learning activities with one another
- Faculty meetings where there is a problem of practice (POP) that staff investigate and bring evidence to share with others so that they can learn from one another
- Coteaching and mentoring

In Pursuit of Collaboration

We know that self-efficacy, collective teacher efficacy, and collaboration are interrelated. For some of us, the word *collaboration* conjures up images of people working together with their sleeves rolled up, making one idea stronger. To others, the word *collaboration* makes them cringe, as they think of yet another meeting where they are asked for their input but know deep down inside that the decision has already been made. Collaboration is sometimes just code for "agree with me so we can move forward, and no one will get hurt."

In order for collaboration to be real and for teachers, students, and parents to feel as though they are a part of a school climate in which they are valued, collaboration needs to include times where we not only learn from one another but also challenge each other's thinking. Kuhn (2015) found,

> More productive collaborations have been identified as those in which participants directly engage one another's thinking. They listen and respond to what their peers say. In less successful collaborations, participants are more likely to work in parallel and ignore or dismiss the other person's contributions. (p. 146)

I believe that our moral purpose as leaders is to challenge our long-held beliefs, build the collective efficacy of staff, help raise the self-efficacy of students and families, and create opportunities in which we learn together through collaboration and a stronger school climate. Michael Fullan (2001), someone I respect greatly for his work in leadership over many decades, writes,

> You don't have to be Mother Theresa to have moral purpose. Some people are deeply passionate about improving life (sometimes to a fault, if they lack one or more of the other four components of leadership: understanding of the change process, strong relationships, knowledge adding, and coherence making

among multiple priorities). Others have a more cognitive approach, displaying less emotion, but still being intensely committed to betterment. Whatever one's style, every leader, to be effective, must have and work on improving his or her moral purpose. (p. 13)

What the Research Says

Research suggests that collaborative leadership can have a positive effect on student learning and achievement. In their longitudinal study involving 192 elementary schools, Hallinger and Heck found that "collaborative leadership positively impacted growth in student learning indirectly through building the academic capacity in schools" (2010, p. 673). The researchers also suggest that there are three important elements to collaborative leadership to assist in its success. Those three areas of focus that Hallinger and Heck found were vision, governance, and resource allocation.

Collaborative Leadership: Elements of Success

- **Vision:** Making decisions to facilitate actions that focus the energy of the school on improving student outcomes and fostering commitment
- **Governance:** Empowering staff and encouraging participation
- **Resource allocation:** Obtaining and allocating resources to support teaching and learning (Hallinger & Heck, 2010, p. 657)

All three of these elements can be achieved by a leader. Authoritative leaders can make sure all three areas are done to compliance, and collaborative leaders can bring together stakeholders to achieve them in a more democratic way. However, this is partly the issue with collaborative leadership and school climate. Not all leaders understand they need to be collaborative and not authoritative.

Huggins, Klar, Hammonds, and Buskey (2016) suggest that any change in leadership style from the norm "requires both principals and teachers to adopt new roles and responsibilities" (p. 204). In order to adopt new roles and responsibilities and work toward a more collaborative school climate, we need to ponder the following questions.

Questions to Ponder When Working Toward a More Collaborative School Climate

- Do we really know what collaboration looks like?
- Do we expect people to collaborate and come up with the same end product?
- Do we expect adults to collaborate and come up with the answer we want as leaders? (That is compliant collaboration and not authentic collaboration.)
- Do we go into collaboration as adults, even when we are doing it with students, and expect to learn something in the process?
- Do we show students, and adults, what collaboration looks like before we have them dive into it?
- Does our school climate support collaboration or compliance?

Collaborative Leadership Framework

This whole idea of leadership, like the many ideas that came before this one, should be about *growth*. For most of us, that is a different way of thinking about leadership than how we learned during our leadership training. For many people, being a leader means you have hit the pinnacle of your career and now need to focus on everyone else's growth.

However, leadership is about growth for others and ourselves. We cannot go back to our first years of leadership, but we certainly don't have to keep making the same mistakes we made that first year. Therefore, collaborative leadership is about growth. It's about fostering the growth of different stakeholders in the school community; it's about fostering our own growth as leaders; and it's about going deeper in our learning and with our relationships. An important aspect to leadership is having a shared understanding of the following:

- Developing and sharing a vision centered on the learning of all students
- Creating and supporting continuous learning opportunities for all staff
- Promoting team learning and collaboration among all staff
- Establishing a culture of inquiry, innovation, and exploration
- Embedding systems for collecting and exchanging knowledge and learning
- Learning with and from the external environment and larger learning system
- Modeling and growing learning leadership (Schleicher, 2008)

In my experience working with school leaders in the United Kingdom, Australia, and North America, I have found some specific types of leaders, which I define as bystanders, regulators, negotiators, and collaborators (DeWitt, 2016a, p. 4). They are all part of what I refer to as the Collaborative Leadership Framework, which is illustrated in Figure 1.1.

The framework is not meant to be a criticism of leaders. It is meant to offer a reflective tool for leaders to study and understand how they might lead, depending on the situation. Those four different types of leadership styles can be more clearly defined the following ways:

Bystanders: These leaders don't define any positive goals, and they don't inspire stakeholders to collaborate. They have low-growth performance and have low-partnership qualities. Teachers work in silos, and the principal remains in her or his office more than being visible.

Figure 1.1   Collaborative Leadership Framework

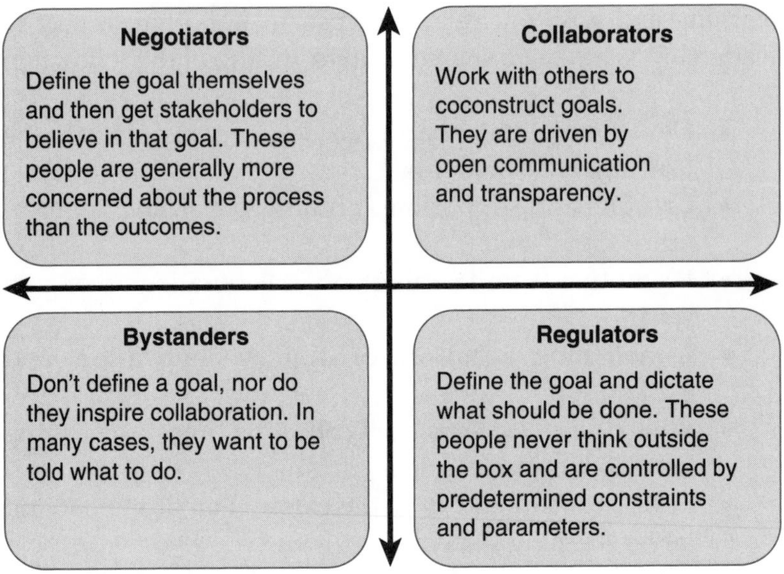

Negotiators

Define the goal themselves and then get stakeholders to believe in that goal. These people are generally more concerned about the process than the outcomes.

Collaborators

Work with others to coconstruct goals. They are driven by open communication and transparency.

Bystanders

Don't define a goal, nor do they inspire collaboration. In many cases, they want to be told what to do.

Regulators

Define the goal and dictate what should be done. These people never think outside the box and are controlled by predetermined constraints and parameters.

Regulators: These leaders define goals for the teacher and the school. Although they have high performance, they control the whole environment. These leaders know what idea they want to exit a meeting with well before they ever enter that meeting. Unfortunately, they do not inspire true partnerships around the school as much as they promote compliance, which ultimately creates a hostile school climate in which teachers wait to be told what to do.

Negotiators: These leaders seem as though they are inspiring collaboration, but what they do is define goals behind closed doors and then slowly make their way around the school or district and get people on board with their ideas. They create coalitions. This works just as long as stakeholders believe in the goals, rather than feel they have to achieve them because they're coming from the top.

Collaborators: These leaders find the perfect balance between inspiring stakeholders to collaborate and coconstructing building- and classroom-level goals. They believe in a high level of transparency and honesty and enjoy a high level of performance because stakeholders feel as though they have a voice in the process.

All leaders spend time in each one of these quadrants because they're situational and often based on our reactions to those situations. For example, when it comes to faculty meetings, some leaders stay in the regulation stage because their staff doesn't always speak up, and the agenda is based on lists of important dates and new compliance items that may be coming from the state or central office.

When it comes to working with families, leaders may be in the bystander stage where they wait for families to come to them when there is an issue, or they allow a parent to barge into their office and vent at them, while they sit behind their desk and pretend to really listen to the issue. After the parent leaves, they tell the teacher to keep a low profile for a little while, and they themselves remain in the office until the dust settles. Day by day, they sit waiting to see if the parent calls back, without reaching out to the parent to see if the matter is resolved.

Given another situation, such as stakeholder meetings that involve different representatives from each grade level or department, leaders in the negotiator stage want everyone to come to consensus. These leaders give the illusion of shared decision-making, when the decision may have already been made before the meeting ever started.

And lastly, leaders may be in the collaboration stage when it comes to teacher observation because they coconstruct a goal with a teacher, so they can provide effective feedback to the teacher during the formal process.

So we have four different situations and four different ways to handle each of those situations. It's very possible to be collaborative in the areas we like to focus on, a bystander in those areas we dislike, a regulator when it comes to school safety protocols, and a negotiator when we really want to get what we want.

Collaborative Leadership Growth Cycle

An important element of understanding which quadrant in the Collaborative Leadership Framework that we may be in at any given time is taking the opportunity to work through a growth cycle. Regardless of where leaders start, whether they spend time in the bystander, regulator, or negotiator stage, they can take the necessary steps to move into the collaboration stage. It is important that leaders who choose to go through this cycle choose one area to work on. Choosing one area is an important distinction because too often our ideas fail when we choose too many in the beginning. If we have too many choices, we choose not to choose at all, so start small. The question leaders need to ask when it comes to their own leadership style is this: Where should I start? Figure 1.2 shows the Collaborative Leadership Growth Cycle.

When it comes to leadership practices, it's important for leaders to understand their current reality. However, we first

Figure 1.2   Collaborative Leadership Growth Cycle

need to start with a goal that has a 0.51 effect size. After reading the introduction, you understand that a 0.51 is well over the hinge point of 0.40.

Collaborative Growth Goal

What area of your leadership would you like to work on? Where do you need to be more collaborative?

- Feedback?
- Parent engagement?
- Student relationships?
- Offering instructional strategies to teachers?

Understand current reality.

- Reflect on where you think you are with that particular goal.

Collect evidence.

- Distribute teacher surveys.
- Review observations you've completed in the past.
- Engineer focus groups.

Be more collaborative.

- Offer one piece of feedback around a goal you created with a teacher before his or her observation.
- Stand out on the sidewalk and try to engage more families—even a few that typically try to blow by you on the sidewalk.
- Go to the Teaching Channel and look for high-impact teaching strategies. Keep those in your toolbox to offer to teachers after an observation or during a walkthrough.

Many leaders don't have the benefit of a coach, so the goal becomes very important in this process because a leader's job encompasses so many different aspects of schooling. They don't often have a clear picture of their current reality because they may lack input from central office administration, without someone directly above them that can shadow them to provide a baseline survey of where their needs are in leadership. My purpose is to help leaders help themselves, and that means goal setting first. That goal can lead them to a better understanding of their current reality in that situation. The following explains each part of the Collaborative Leadership Growth Cycle.

Goal Setting (Effect Size of 0.51)

The ultimate goal should be to become a collaborative leader by focusing on one specific situation in their leadership. Remember, often leaders believe they have to become a collaborative leader in every aspect of their leadership, especially after reading books like this. They don't. In order to change traditional practice, we all have to start small and not be too lofty. Think of it as a grassroots effort to change our leadership style. So the bottom line is to choose one area of leadership that you want to change the most.

Let's look at the faculty meeting (DeWitt, 2014) for an example. Leaders want to change the way they run faculty meetings and make them less about checking off a list of items teachers need to complete and more about making those meetings about professional development. Therefore, their goal is to flip their faculty meetings. Flipping is the process of sending an article, blog, or video to teachers about three days ahead of the meeting so they can read or watch it and come to the meeting with some surface-level knowledge in order to have deeper conversations with colleagues at the meeting. By flipping the meeting this way, you will build collective teacher efficacy.

Current Reality

The next step for leaders is to understand the current reality in that specific situation. What has been their leadership style leading up to this point? Have they been bystanders in the process, where faculty make negative comments about how they can't do the things on the list and the leader remains quiet, hoping that the complaints will stop? Or have they been regulators, where they go through the list of tasks on their faculty agenda and tell staff by when they must be completed?

It is important for leaders to understand their faculty meeting leadership style because that typically contributes to whether they have a positive or negative school climate. If they regulate the meeting, it is most likely that their teachers feel regulated during most of their day, which contributes to a more hostile school climate.

Evidence Gathering

After leaders understand their current reality, they will do some evidence gathering to help them reflect on past practice and will understand how to move forward. Without using evidence, we are just remembering it the way we *think* it happened and not necessarily the way it *did* happen. This evidence-gathering mission that leaders go through needs to include artifacts such as surveys or interviews with a well-rounded group that provide the leader with honest answers. Clearly, this will take a positive school climate, something I will focus on in this book. It is important to choose one or two ways to collect evidence to get an idea of how the faculty meeting felt to the teachers sitting on the receiving end.

Stop. Collaborate and Listen!

As a way to gather evidence, provide a simple anonymous exit survey after the faulty meeting. Teachers and staff can leave it in an "Exit Survey" box within 24 hours after the meeting ends. Ask the following questions:

- What did you learn at the meeting?
- How will you use it?
- What were you hoping to learn?
- What would you like us to do differently next time?

If you want to step it up a bit and make it more anonymous, send out a link to a Google Survey where you can ask the same questions and keep track of the data it provides for you regarding faculty meetings.

Action Step

After leaders go through the evidence-gathering portion of the Collaborative Leadership Growth Cycle, it's important to choose a next step. What will the next step be? Perhaps, the leader has a school stakeholder group (that involves grade-level representatives or chairs from different departments) already in place, and they can talk with the group about coconstructing a goal for the next three faculty meetings. I've met leaders who get excited about making faculty meetings about professional development (PD), and they want the stakeholder group to come up with a yearlong plan. Try not to do that. Often when leaders do a yearlong plan around faculty meetings and PD, they hit the implementation dip (Fullan, 2001) part-way through and drop the idea altogether, so choose a faculty focus for the next three months and then build on that momentum. Celebrate the small successes.

Leaders often have questions about coconstructing goals for faculty meetings and the feeling of being caught in the middle between central office initiatives and the needs of teachers. One of the ways leaders can make the collaborative growth cycle more impactful is to involve another colleague who can hold the leader responsible for achieving the goal. We often do better with a goal when we have a critical friend who can help keep us invested. Research that shows reciprocal teaching has a 0.74 effect size (Hattie, 2012a). It is an influence on learning that works for adults and students.

Lastly, it's important to remember that we shouldn't reinvent the wheel, and if the district initiative is going to stay the district initiative (and hopefully leaders and teachers had a say in it), we should do our best to focus on that district initiative. If we stick with the same faculty meeting goal for our Collaborative Leadership Growth Cycle, let's use an example of how a district initiative can be addressed in the faculty meeting, which contributes to a school climate that focuses on learning. The following is an example of a possible initiative that school districts adopt.

District Initiative: *Literacy*

Stakeholder Group: What are high-quality literacy practices?

October Faculty Meeting: Staff members bring their best literacy practice and are prepared to have dialogue around those practices.

- The leader sends one article or blog out to staff regarding best practices in literacy. This will help prime the pump when it comes to dialogue. Timperely and colleagues (2007) found that the best professional development challenges the beliefs of staff, so leaders should find something that will challenge beliefs.
- The leader looks for the common theme among the ideas shared by staff.
- The leader and staff discuss the common themes and come up with two or three to explore in the next faculty meeting.

November Faculty Meeting: Dive deeper into the *shared* practices from October.

- Facilitate Q&A around what was shared at the last meeting (reflection time).
  - How do we engage students with these practices?
  - What is our current reality?
  - How many teachers use these practices?
  - What does that look like?
  - If we could paint a picture of the perfect literacy lesson, what would that look like?
  - Partner with a colleague from another grade level to discuss.

The ultimate goal where the cycle is concerned is to choose an area in which leaders can be more collaborative at the end. I chose the faculty meeting because it's one of those areas that often is a waste of time for teachers because most of the items spoken about could have been sent out in an e-mail. However, some other ideas include how teachers and leaders can engage with families, the teacher observation process, or the positive ways we talk with students. This focus is not only on learning but on how teachers and staff can focus on authentic collaboration as opposed to compliant engagement.

If leaders are looking for goals to work on in their leadership practices, there are six influences (DeWitt, 2016a) that I believe will help any leader be more impactful.

Six Influences That Matter Most

Instructional leadership (0.42): Instructional leadership is highly important to how a school community focuses on learning. High-quality instructional leaders coconstruct goals with their staff to provide professional development that helps teachers understand what the best high-impact learning strategies are, as well as helps teachers understand the important part gathering evidence plays in driving instruction.

Collective teacher efficacy (CTE; 1.57): CTE describes how much more powerful teachers can be when they work together to improve student learning. In order to build CTE, we need to have an understanding of self-efficacy. Self-efficacy (0.63) describes the confidence we have in ourselves to achieve our goals. Unfortunately, there are teachers who suffer from a low level of self-efficacy, which means that they do not believe they have an impact on the learning happening in their classrooms. It is important that school leaders work collaboratively to build the collective efficacy of teachers and students.

Professional development (PD; 0.51): Timperley, Wilson, Baraar, and Fung (2007) state that if we want PD to be effective it needs to meet the following characteristics:

- Occurs over a long period of time (3–5 years)
- Involves external experts
- Deeply engages teachers
- Challenges teachers' existing beliefs
- Encourages teachers to talk to each other about teaching
- Provides opportunities for teachers to learn within the school structure
- Has support of administrators

Feedback (0.75): Feedback has three levels: (1) task feedback for new learning; (2) process-level feedback when the student or teacher has some degree of proficiency; and (3) self-regulation when the person receiving the feedback has a high degree of proficiency. Effective feedback can only be given when it's wrapped around learning intentions and success criteria.

Assessment-capable learners (1.44): *Assessment-capable learners* can be defined as those students who can tell you where they are, how they got there, and where they're going next. Some schools call them *self-directed learners.*

Family engagement (0.49): Collaborative leadership is about building dialogue with families. Communication between families and schools needs to be two-sided. In addition to letting families know how they can support the school and students, we also need to explicitly ask them how we can help support them.

In Figure 1.3, you will see a rubric that I created for leaders, teacher leaders, or instructional coaches to use to reflect on their leadership practices around the six influences that matter most. However, the first section revolves around school climate because that is the plate that everything else sits on. Without a supportive school climate, it will be difficult for the six influences to reach their full potential.

A leader can choose one of the six influences that matter most from the rubric as a goal to work on during the Collaborative Leadership Growth Cycle. For example, family engagement may be an area where leaders find themselves in the regulation stage because they are always putting out one-sided communication rather than building dialogue. In the current reality stage of the growth cycle, leaders can send out surveys to parents to get feedback on their level of engagement with families. Additionally, on the survey the leader can ask for examples of better ways to communicate with the community and use those examples. The important thing to remember is that doing a survey is easy, but putting suggestions into action and then making those actions a habit is the hard part.

Figure 1.3 Collaborative Leadership Rubric

Collaborative Leadership Rubric	Bystander	Regulator	Negotiator	Collaborator
School climate	Has stakeholder groups only if mandated by the district, but the meetings focus more on tasks and being reactive rather than goals and being proactive. Sporadically communicates to parents about events and important dates they need to know. Has district-mandated safeguards for students, but doesn't always follow through on them.	Has stakeholder groups that achieve the goal set by the leader. Creates one-sided communication with parents. Offers curriculum and safeguards that are inclusive of all students, regardless of race, gender, religion, ability, and sexual orientation, because they want all students to feel safe and because it is district-mandated.	Has stakeholder groups, some of which include parents and students, that ultimately will achieve the goal set by the leader. Creates mostly one-sided communication with parents. Offers curriculum and safeguards that are inclusive of all students, regardless of race, gender, religion, ability, and sexual orientation.	Has several stakeholder groups, some of which include parents and students, that focus on coconstructed goals. Surveys families for feedback on communication, as well as offers curriculum and safeguards that are inclusive of all students, regardless of race, gender, religion, ability, and sexual orientation.
Instructional leadership	Leaves instructional strategies up to the teacher. Teacher observations offer little to no feedback to teachers.	Creates protocols to make sure mandated curriculum is being followed. Checks lesson plans on a rotating basis to ensure teachers are pacing appropriately. Observations are based on district-mandated curriculum that must be followed and focus on evaluative feedback around issues in the classroom that need to be improved.	Engages in conversations to make sure that teachers are following top-down mandates. Observations focus on goals that the leader wants the teacher to establish, and the feedback provided to teachers in the postconversation focuses on those goals, as well as other parts that can be improved.	Coconstructs goals with teachers and staff at the beginning of the year and encourages teachers to do the same with students. Preobservation and postobservations are collaborative in nature and the feedback provided is based on the learning intentions and success criteria established around the teacher's goal.

Collaborative Leadership Rubric	Bystander	Regulator	Negotiator	Collaborator
Professional development	Teachers are free to do whatever professional development they choose as long as there is money in the budget or the PD is free and on the teacher's own time. Faculty meetings revolve around important dates and times. The quicker the faculty meeting, the better!	Teachers are mandated to take part in districtwide professional development, and what they learned must be seen in the classroom. Teachers are free to do PD on their own time as long as it fits into district goals as well as adheres to mandates and accountability measures.	Teachers are mandated to take part in districtwide professional development, and what they learned must be seen in the classroom. Teachers are free to do PD on their own time. Teachers are encouraged to share their new learning at faculty meetings and PLCs.	Teachers have a mixture of responsibilities. They need to attend district-mandated PD but are also encouraged to attend Edcamps and share their best practices at faculty meetings. Faculty meetings are flipped in order to provide teachers and staff with deeper learning around the coconstructed goals and common themes of teachers and staff.
Feedback	Provides praise and little constructive feedback. Praise is important, but it doesn't replace feedback.	Provides evaluative feedback after observations and walkthroughs based on what the leader believes is important.	Provides evaluative, coaching, and appreciative feedback after observations and walkthroughs based on what the leader believes is important.	Provides evaluative, coaching, and appreciative feedback after observations and walkthroughs based on a coconstructed goal with the teacher. Additionally, this leader understands how people receive feedback (Stone & Heen, 2015) as well and takes that into consideration when working with teachers.

(Continued)

Figure 1.3 (Continued)

Collaborative Leadership Rubric	Bystander	Regulator	Negotiator	Collaborator
Collective teacher efficacy	Teachers mostly work in silos. However, if teachers want to work in groups, that is fine as well. The leader appreciates that teachers will work cooperatively but does not necessarily need to see evidence that it's working.	Teachers can either work in silos or they can work in cooperative grade-level or department-specific groups. It all depends on what the leader wants, and any of the work that is being done needs to follow district mandates, and teachers must provide evidence that what they are doing is working.	"As a leader, along with my teacher leaders and coaches, I have a deep understanding of teaching and learning. Please feel free to join us in the conversation and work with us toward that goal, but unless you fit into our present understanding, your ideas will not be fully considered. However, if you do agree with us, you will be an important part of the team."	"As a leader, I understand the research behind self-efficacy, and I will help build a relationship with you because I respect your voice and expertise. There will be equal give and take, where I will listen to your ideas as well as share mine. However, I will ask you for evidence so you can prove your strategies are working, and I will provide you with the same courtesy. It is my goal to establish stakeholder groups and PLCs that maximize the involvement of all teachers."
Assessment-capable learners	"Students need to learn the curriculum for their grade level and perform well on state tests and districtwide growth measures. However, some students may just be	"Students need to learn the curriculum for their grade level and perform well on state tests and districtwide growth measures. Additionally, I know that	"Students need to learn the curriculum for their grade level and perform well on state tests and districtwide growth measures. We should look at Hattie's top-ten	"How do students learn best? How do we, and our students, know what makes a good learner a good learner? We need to answer those questions first, and then look

Collaborative Leadership Rubric	Bystander	Regulator	Negotiator	Collaborator
Assessment-capable learners (continued)	unteachable (though we know that's not politically correct to say). By the way, who is John Hattie?"	Hattie has a list of top-ten influences, and we need to put those into action. That does not mean I have done a great deal of research on Hattie, but I know his name and have heard other schools are using his work."	influences and use those. I want to see those in action when I observe students."	at our growth measures and research more about formative assessment to make sure that we are meeting the needs of our students in real time. This will help us understand our current reality when it comes to student learning and then choose the influences by Hattie that will help us meet our goal. Additionally, we should focus on having a better understanding of why those specific influences worked in Hattie's research and try our best to replicate that."
Family engagement	"Don't call us, we'll call you."	"Here is what you need to do to support your child."	"Here is what you need to do to support your child, but we are open to your feedback. However, you may not see any evidence that we listened to your feedback because we are more concerned with our goals."	"Let's work together. Please provide us feedback in how we are communicating. What is your goal for your child when it comes to academic and social-emotional learning?"

In the End

In order to understand our school community, we should first seek to understand ourselves as leaders, and that begins with looking at our leadership styles. How often do we spend time in the mindset of a collaborative leader, and how often do we find ourselves in the mindset of a regulator, negotiator, or bystander? It's important to understand that just as teachers can suffer from a low level of self-efficacy, leaders can suffer from that same issue as well. After so many years of accountability, mandates, and initiative fatigue, leaders can find themselves feeling lost within their positions and retreating to their offices where they can hide from issues. To combat that feeling, try to move forward with one goal because as I once heard Michael Fullan say at a conference in New Zealand, "Just because you're stuck with their policies doesn't mean you need to be stuck with their mindset." It's really important to understand that no matter how hard we try to hide, those issues will find us, and we need to be prepared. Just remember that this book is about starting small, creating a goal, and understanding your current reality—and inspiring others to do the same.

ACTION STEPS

- What goal will you work on?
  - Faculty meeting focus
  - Teacher observation
  - Parent communication
  - Student voice

- What is your current reality when it comes to that issue you are focusing on?
  - Negotiator, bystander, or regulator

- How will you gather evidence?
  - Student or teacher surveys

- How will you address the evidence/findings with staff?
- How will you know that you have reached the collaboration stage?

DISCUSSION QUESTIONS

- When have you experienced the four leadership styles mentioned in this chapter?
- How might self-efficacy be enhanced in your school?
  - How does it affect the adults in the school community?
- In what ways can you begin working on the collective efficacy of staff?
- How do you meet, model, and motivate?
  - If you could paint a picture of it, what would it look like?

TIM AND TRUDY

- What would Tim need to do to make his leadership stronger?
  - What information could he use from Chapter 1 to make that happen?
- Where would Trudy need to begin to start working on her leadership skills?

Collaborative Leadership Reflection Tool

The following are some reflective questions to answer (also found in the Appendix on page 179). Answer them honestly in the comfort of a private setting. If you have a critical friend with whom to complete this, answer the questions and then discuss with her or him. This is not a judgment, but a reflective tool.

I'm not overly concerned with the goals of my staff as long as they don't get in the way of the task I need to complete in my office.	True	False
I don't know the goals of each staff member in my building.	True	False
I prefer to wait for staff, teachers, students, or families to contact me about an issue, even if I know about it first.	True	False
I prefer to sit back and listen to staff members during conversations to hear their line of thinking.	True	False
Meeting central-office needs is the most important aspect of my job.	True	False
I like to walk into a meeting with one idea and walk out with the same one.	True	False
I expect the notes from each PLC, grade level, or department meeting to make sure people are doing their jobs.	True	False
I set goals with each teacher before a formal observation so I know where I should aim my feedback.	True	False
I know I will find something for the teacher to improve on before I enter their classroom for an observation.	True	False
I check the lesson plans of all of my teachers on a consistent basis and hand them back with feedback they can read.	True	False
I discuss lesson plans with teachers on a consistent basis, and they give me insight into what students are learning so I can provide them with the best feedback possible.	True	False
I need to get the answers to my questions on a regular basis.	True	False
I listen to other people's concerns fully before I provide my insight.	True	False

I try my best to say *our* faculty and *our* school instead of *my* faculty and *my* school.	True	False
I do not have to have all of the answers before I walk into the meeting because I know the collective power of the staff will come up with the best solution to our problem.	True	False
I often have meetings after a meeting because I want to further explain my goal.	True	False
I steer the conversation with staff toward my idea, but in the end, I want them to think it's actually their idea so they're on board.	True	False
I need to have all of the answers before I go into an individual or group meeting.	True	False
I don't really like to question initiatives coming from central office.	True	False
I like to build consensus.	True	False
I am OK with faculty asking me any question in a faculty meeting. I prefer to discuss the elephant in the room and come out with a better understanding of the mindset of staff.	True	False
I don't mind respectful confrontation, as long as it leads to a better place for both of us.	True	False
It is important for me to foster opportunities for all staff members to share their voices.	True	False
I make sure that those teachers who dominate meetings understand that everyone has the right to talk.	True	False

Leadership Style: _____

2

School Climate

Setting Up a Safe Space to Collaborate

A member of the next generation of leaders may be the quiet person in your next meeting who has not spoken up because you have not asked a question.

—Douglas Reeves

Collaboration is not a new word for our vernacular. It has been around for many years. It began to take on a much larger role in education since the Partnership for 21st Century Learning (P21) introduced it as one of the 4Cs of 21st century skills, along with creativity, critical thinking, and communication (2016, p. 1). The 4Cs are brilliant and will help students be prepared for college and the workplace. However, are they really new to the 21st century? No, but they have been an important catalyst to our discussions over the last decade about what our students need.

One problem with introducing 21st century skills—such as collaboration—in classrooms is that schools focused on the 4Cs for students but then realized the adults charged with teaching those students may not know how to collaborate, or had been given little time to collaborate themselves. Preservice teaching programs do not always teach students how to collaborate with one another as much as they assign a project and force collaboration among students. In order to effectively teach students the 4Cs, we adults must have a good grasp on them as well. We must understand the nuances of working with others and that some group members come to collaboration with a high level of self-efficacy while others come with a low level of self-efficacy.

We also have to understand that some group collaborators who are the loudest are not necessarily the ones who are bringing the best ideas, and those who are sometimes the quietest are our diamonds in the rough. And that is why climate—both classroom climate and school climate—are so important. In fact, climate should be the fifth C (see Figure 2.1)! Without an engaging and supportive school climate, schools will never

Figure 2.1   21st Century Learning Pie Chart

Source: Adapted from Partnership for 21st Century Learning (www.p21.org).

dive deeply into the other 4Cs. And without a proper school climate, innovative practices will never meet their full potential. Additionally, with a proper school climate teachers, leaders, and students can find their way through even the most difficult situations.

We know that students come from various types of difficult situations, which is why this fifth C—climate—is becoming increasingly important. School leaders and staff are as concerned about the social-emotional health of students as much as they are concerned for the academic learning that is necessary. They go hand in hand, and there is some disturbing research out there that shows how concerned with social-emotional health we need to be. In fact, the World Health Organization (WHO) offers a staggering prediction:

One in four people in the world will be affected by mental or neurological disorders at some point in their lives. Around 450 million people currently suffer from such conditions, placing mental disorders among the leading causes of ill-health and disability worldwide. (2001b, para. 1)

Sadly, two-thirds of people will never get assistance (WHO, 2001b), and this has a profound impact on our school climate because this statistic involves students, staff, and families.

Collaborative leadership involves fostering a school climate in which we talk about issues affecting our world, while having a strong focus on social-emotional health as well. The National School Climate Center (n.d.) defines *school climate* in this way:

The quality and character of school life and experiences that reflects norms, values, interpersonal relationships, teaching, learning and leadership practices, and organizational structures; a sustainable, positive school climate fosters youth development and learning necessary for a productive, contributing, and satisfying life in a democratic society. (para. 3)

School climate improves student achievement and a student's sense of belonging (Hughes & Pickeral, 2013), and most leaders would say they want a positive school climate. However, our actions regarding school climate are just as important as our words. Saying we want a positive one isn't enough. It begins from the moment students, teachers, and parents walk in the main lobby, and it involves our secretaries, main office staff, and what we have hanging in the foyer and on the hallway walls. Taking action to make sure we have a positive and inclusive school climate means those actions include all students, regardless of race, religion, sexual orientation, or gender. That is not as easy as we may think because it involves having policies, codes of conduct, clubs, and curriculum that protect those students.

Ten Recommendations for Creating a Positive School Climate

1. Raise awareness of social climate characteristics, standards, and research to ensure agreement by education stakeholders.

2. Adopt school climate standards to ensure systemwide integration with focus on safety, relationships, teaching and learning, and physical environment.

3. Create policies that allocate resources to effectively implement school climate assessments, analyses, and improvement.

4. Conduct regular assessments of school climate using research-based tools.

5. Identify specific intended outcomes and impacts of school climate reform and effective assessment measures.

6. Focus on shared leadership and diverse perspectives, as they provide the foundation for sustainability.

7. Create leadership opportunities for all students to contribute to school climate reform.

8. Promote professional development that increases school climate knowledge and skills through professional learning communities.

9. Integrate instructional strategies that engage students in developing academic, social, civic, and career competencies.

10. Support positive relationships among students, among adults, and between students and adults in school and community. (Pickeral, 2016, para. 3)

An important aspect of most of these recommendations is the need for dialogue around what many might consider tough topics, such as race, gender, religion, and sexual orientation. These issues often play themselves out in school. However, even among adults we choose to ignore the conversations in the hope that they will go away. There are very few safe topics anymore. In order to really move forward and make our school climates places where we can increase dialogue, we have to stop avoiding certain conversations because when we do, it limits our learning.

School Climate: Why Avoiding Tough Conversations Limits Our Learning

Peter DeWitt (2016d)

November 15, 2016
Finding Common Ground Blog—blogs.edweek.org

School climate seems to be gaining popularity right now. I've heard leaders say they want to focus on it, but there isn't enough time and they can't handle another thing on their plate. This is flawed thinking because school climate is the plate that everything else sits on.

We cannot get students to think critically, be creative, work in collaboration, and communicate (P21's 4Cs) if we have a school climate that doesn't address the tough situations that happen in schools for our minoritized populations. Minoritized students are those who are pushed into feeling like the minority by another more dominant group.

(Continued)

(Continued)

Minoritized students rarely see images in school that look like them, have teachers who read books on topics that address their needs, or hear common language that makes them feel included in the school community.

If we're going to talk about school climate, then we need to be addressing the needs of minoritized groups.

Sometimes this happens because teachers feel that these are tough topics and they know their leaders won't support them when there is parent pushback. Other times these minoritized groups are seen through the lens of a deficit model. And lastly, these topics are ignored because the adults in the school don't even think about addressing them.

School climate means we talk about these issues.

At-Risk Populations

Ruth Berkowitz and colleagues (2017) recently highlighted the work of Andrew Halpin and Don Croft, who are described as the "pioneers of research on school climate." According to Berkowitz,

> Halpin and Croft maintained that climate is the "personality" of the school, expressing the collective perception of teachers of school routine and thereby influencing their attitudes and behaviors. Their definition was based on the measure of a school's openness and assumed six prototypes of school climate. (p. 425)

Those six prototypes that Halpin and Croft (1963) researched are the following:

- Peer sensitivity
- Disruptiveness
- Teacher–student interactions
- Achievement orientation
- Support for diversity
- Safety

Let's take for example, a student in the LGBT community and the 4Cs (critical thinking, creativity, collaboration, communication)—the 21st century skills that have been so important. In the Gay, Lesbian, & Straight Education Network's (GLSEN) *2013 National School Climate Survey*, Kosciw, Greytak,

Palmer, and Boesen (2014) found that "55.5% of LGBT students felt unsafe at school because of their sexual orientation, and 37.8% because of their gender expression" (p. xvi). Furthermore, "30.3% of LGBT students missed at least one entire day of school in the past month because they felt unsafe or uncomfortable, and over a tenth (10.6%) missed four or more days in the past month" (p. xvi).

Those statistics illustrate the need for leaders and teachers to establish an inclusive and safe school climate because no one can be a productive member of a collaborative group if he or she feels unsafe in school. I mean, if we truly want to get the best out of all our students, then we have to address their needs so they feel as though they can contribute to the larger group.

If LGBT students have been harassed or bullied within their school, even if no one within their collaborative group is responsible, it is possible that those students are less likely to contribute. Chances are they may be skipping school on days when the collaboration is taking place. *All of this contributes to school climate.*

Let's examine a more international issue, and that is the indigenous population within our schools. In Australia, there are Aboriginal students; in New Zealand, there are Pacific Island students; and in North America, we have Native American students. Do they see images that are representative of their culture in their schools? Do they feel as though they are valued members of their school climate?

In the End

School climate is one of those areas that we talk about briefly but often say we don't have time to examine in-depth because there are too many things on our plate. Then we jump into the next 21st century initiative to better prepare our students for the workplace and forget to have the tough conversations that help all of our students feel as though they belong.

If students are to learn how to work in collaboration with other students—and not just the ones they choose to sit and work with—then they need to understand the experiences of *all* the students within their group. In life, we can't always work with others who are like-minded, nor should we want that as our goal because it limits the learning potential of the situation.

(Continued)

(Continued)

Figure 2.2   Essential Components of School Climate

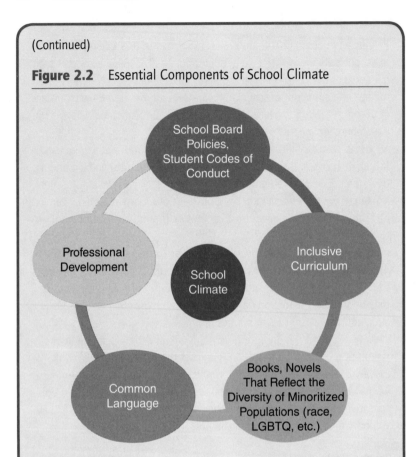

If we have not held conversations, read books, or held classroom discussions about cultural proficiency that include images to represent our whole student population, will we really ever get them to reach beyond their potential?

Do your textbooks, novels, curriculum, movies, and images around your school represent everyone within your school community? Will all of your students ever excel at the 4Cs if we haven't properly addressed the important fifth C—climate?

If you really want an inclusive and safe school climate for all students, then the following need to be addressed and supported (see Figure 2.2):

Safeguards: Student codes of conduct and school board policies are in place that safeguard all students regardless of race, gender, sexual orientation, and religious beliefs. Not only do those documents have protective language, but leaders and teachers follow through on them.

Inclusive curriculum: All students are represented in the curriculum taught in schools.

Inclusive books and novels: There are books within classrooms and the library that represent all students in the school.

Common language: Staff members understand and use acronyms such as *LGBTQ* and phrases such as *minoritized populations*.

Professional development (PD): Provide PD to help all staff members know what to say, how to say it, and how to move forward.

Why Does School Climate Matter?

In the introduction to the book, I provided two stories about two very different leaders. We read about Tim, who is the high school principal who seems to work collaboratively with his large school. We can imagine that Tim most likely welcomes those tough conversations that are needed to provide a more supportive school climate. Perhaps he approaches the conversations by providing resources ahead of a faculty meeting for staff to read so they enter the meeting more prepared. Or perhaps it's in how he approaches the conversation—by listening more than he talks.

We can speculate that Trudy, who seems to regulate every move of staff and students, is not the type of person who likes to talk through tough conversations because they make her feel uncomfortable. However, if we view Trudy through a self-efficacy lens, it's possible to understand that she doesn't feel comfortable because she doesn't have all the answers to the issue and feels very insecure regarding those issues.

Regardless of which administrator you identify with, you can imagine why school climate matters so much and how the approach of the leader can have a massive impact on the climate of the school. In one story, teachers probably feel comfortable enough to take risks, and in the other, teachers may be too scared to take a risk.

Additionally, if we keep in mind the six prototypes—peer sensitivity, disruptiveness, teacher–student interactions, achievement orientation, support for diversity, and safety (Halpin & Croft, 1963)—leaders need to understand that part of their job is to make sure all students feel engaged and valued. You could tell in Trudy's story that she was more likely to question students' motives in the hallway rather than ask them how they are doing; but you could probably tell that Tim would be more likely to make students feel engaged and valued. If students do not feel engaged and valued, they will not reach their potential at school, are at risk of dropping out or being a behavior issue, and will become disenchanted with school.

We may believe that high-poverty schools are in most need of a school climate redo, but even high-achieving schools need to look at their climates. In an e-mail correspondence, Terrance Mootz, an assistant superintendent in Cicero, Illinois, wrote,

> School climate is such a multifaceted construct. It is influenced by the individual, group, and organizational history, yet impacts policy, school improvement, teacher practice, and, ultimately, student learning. The gap between research and operational implementation, in many instances, is socially unjust for the students and families that could most benefit from strong climate. (December 2016)

Mootz went on to write, "Conversely, those schools with strong achievement may be in the most need for school climate overhaul because they may be focused on output and are not developing the student as a whole" (2016). The tough conversations we often avoid are the ones we should be exploring because they play themselves out in school.

DeWitt and Slade found that

> a positive school climate is an environment in which all people—not just adults or educators—are engaged and respected and where students, families, and educators work together to develop, live, and contribute to a shared school vision. (2014, p. 9)

Stop. Collaborate and Listen!

Create a Climate Plan

Use your building stakeholder group to create a school climate plan.

Focus

The top five areas of a school climate are the following:

- Curriculum
- School code of conduct
- Professional development
- Common language
- Literature

Evidence

Collect evidence on all five areas to get a sense of your current reality:

- Does the evidence show that all students of varying race, sexual orientation, ability, gender, and the like are represented within all five areas?
- If not, what can you do to make sure that area is representative of all students (e.g., schedule PD regarding more inclusive language to use in school; establish a school code of conduct that provides safeguards for all students regardless of sexual orientation, ability, gender, race, religion, etc.)?

(Continued)

(Continued)

Learn

Make a list of the necessary learning that will be involved:

- What new learning is involved to provide a common understanding among the stakeholder group (e.g., professional development, articles, blogs, other resources)?
- Who is responsible for creating the learning opportunities?

Action

Creating actionable steps is important to the process.

- What action can the stakeholder group take to close the gap?

Collaborative Leadership Framework for Teachers

The discussions needed to create a climate plan will never happen until all stakeholders feel safe to express their opinions, and not everyone does. It's usually a small group of individuals who feel comfortable pushing the tough conversations forward, and that often means that there is a serious lack of collaborative conversations taking place. Therefore, the Collaborative Leadership Framework is not just for school leaders. During any given collaborative process, there are several mindsets that are present. Those mindsets fit into the Collaborative Leadership Framework as well as a leader's mindset fits into the framework, so it's equally as important for teachers, specialists, and school staff to all play a part in the collaboration (see Figure 2.3).

The following are the roles taken on by the teachers:

Bystander: Just tell me what you need me to do, and I will make my students do it that way.

Regulator: This is exactly what you need to do. I make my students do it this way, so it's correct.

Negotiator: I like how you're doing it that way, but I'm doing it this way and it seems to work better with my students.

Collaborator: I have some ideas on how to start, but I think together we can come up with a better way for our students.

This issue that once only depicted the different types of leaders within a school community, now helps to illustrate the teacher leaders within that community as well. And this is very much aligned with school climate. Leithwood and colleagues (2004) found, "Teachers' motivation and work setting, however, seem much more susceptible to leadership influence and so have significant effects on student achievement" (p. 554).

Figure 2.3 Collaborative Leadership Framework

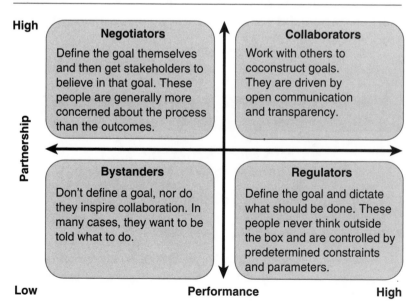

In order to build collective efficacy, which Hattie's (2012a) research shows to have a 1.57 effect size, we need to bring all teachers to a more collaborative mindset, which means that we need to raise their level of self-efficacy (0.63) through elevating their teacher voice, coconstructing goals with them, focusing on the positive practices they display in the classroom (e.g., teacher–student relationships, teaching strategies, classroom climate), and listening to their needs. Collaborative leaders understand Leithwood's research around motivation and work setting, and they know that one of the best places to address these issues is through their regular stakeholder meetings, such as faculty meetings and professional learning communities (PLCs).

A positive school climate is one in which teachers and students have a voice in the process; they challenge the thinking of each other and work hard to stay in the role of collaborators as opposed to the other roles of regulator, negotiator, and bystander.

To provide an example of what that may look like at the teacher level, Sarah Philp, a former principal educational psychologist, provides the following vignette to help illustrate the work that took place in her school consortium to foster teacher voice, build collective efficacy, and ultimately impact student learning.

Practitioner's Voice

Fostering Collective Efficacy
to Increase Student Ownership

Sarah Philp, Former Principal Educational Psychologist
Midlothian Council
Director of Learning, Osiris Educational

Midlothian Council is one of 32 council areas in Scotland and is located south of Edinburgh. It consists of two nurseries, 34 primary schools, and six secondary schools. The Educational Psychology Service consists of a team of seven educational psychologists who work to make a positive difference in the lives of all children and young people.

As a principal educational psychologist (PEP), it will probably come as no surprise that my approach to collaboration has been both relational and driven by evidence. There has been no road map for this journey, and there have been many times when I have worried I have gotten it wrong, but then I visit a school or talk to a teacher or school leader and I am provided with the evidence I need to keep focused. We were ambitious in our approach as we focused not just on one school, but on all schools and all teachers.

Nurturing collective efficacy has become a way of being and thinking as much as it is doing; ultimately, it is relational in nature. I have consistently asked myself, How is what I am doing helping to build capacity across the system? Our capacity comes through our professional, human, and collective efficacy.

Getting to where we are now has taken, quite literally, thousands of actions with a relentless focus on nurturing collective efficacy; every conversation is an opportunity. We "engage in dialogue, not monologue" (Hattie, 2012b). While we have fully embraced technology and social media tools such as Twitter for sharing ideas and practice, nothing quite compares with a conversation. Personal communication and finding the time for people builds individual engagement and motivation for the work that needs to be done. Every conversation is an opportunity to get feedback about how we are doing and what else is needed or what needs to change.

I had the great privilege of working with a small group of teachers from across Midlothian who came together to act as a focus group for me. I asked them to commit to three meetings, and two years later, the group still meets to explore the opportunities and challenges we face within our approach to Hattie's Visible Learning. These teachers provide a chain of influence and communication with other teachers in their schools and clusters. Teacher voice needs to be heard and embraced—we all know how empowering it feels to be listened to and how frustrating the opposite is.

(Continued)

(Continued)

Effective teacher professional learning has a significant impact on outcomes for pupils. Using the key principles from research, we have prioritized professional learning for teachers and ensured that this continues to be strategically resourced while listening to what teachers want and need. This is not just about a "wish list" of presenters or opportunities, but it is also about using evidence to inform what is needed based on the needs of our pupils and therefore the needs of our teachers and support staff.

Over the last few years, we have developed a range of professional learning opportunities for teachers that contribute to our understanding and development of the principles and practice of Visible Learning. Teachers have come together from across schools and sectors to learn together, to support and challenge one another. This has in turn created a foundation for more teacher-led professional learning such as the following:

- Reading groups
- Blogging
- Visits between schools
- Walkthroughs
- Practitioner enquiry
- A recent "pedagoo" event

Developing a culture of trust and openness in which teachers share their work and most importantly their impact with others has allowed us to better use our internal resources, feeding our potential for collective efficacy.

Learning from and with others has not been restricted to Midlothian. Through Twitter, we connected with schools in England and Wales, and the hashtag #VLNetworkUK emerged, as well as the opportunity to visit other schools. In March 2016, we hosted a visit of over 50 educators from across the United Kingdom, which gave us the opportunity to see ourselves through the eyes of others.

The feedback we received confirmed that we are focusing on the right things, the things that have the biggest impact. The cycle of feedback has been important in building motivation and collaboration toward a common goal. Our visitors found these things to be true:

- The enthusiasm of staff was infectious.
- Collaboration was evident throughout and was based on relational trust.

- There was a culture in which teachers are learners too.
- There was a shared language and framework for thinking about learning and impact.
- Twitter and blogging are useful tools for sharing practice, ideas, and impact across schools locally and nationally.

Through our efforts to build collective efficacy, we now have a shared framework and a shared language of learning across all schools and beyond. We brought further coherence to this through our vision of a "Midlothian Learner" (see Figure 2.4), our shared aspirations for all our learners. This allows each school community (including pupils and families) to focus on the actions most relevant to their context (based on their evidence) within a shared vision for all Midlothian learners.

We have external validation that we have successfully shifted the focus from teaching to learning, our core business. Teachers and school leaders regularly tell me that this is why they came into teaching in the first place, that they are excited and motivated by the impact

Figure 2.4   Characteristics of a Midlothian Learner

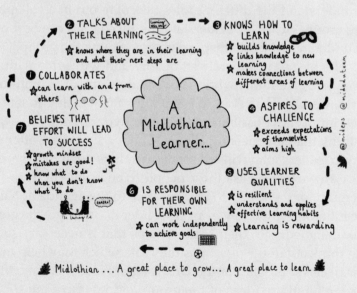

(Continued)

(Continued)

that they are having in their classroom, their school, or their learning community.

Developing collective efficacy requires us to maintain and continuously build momentum. We need to bring this to every action and interaction. Most of all, we need to care because this passion is what brought us here in the first place; it is what keeps us going and it engages others—it can be infectious and motivating. Don't leave collective efficacy to chance—make it your intention.

Creating Collaborative Conversations

There are many other ways to inspire collaboration among staff at faculty meetings. All of this is dependent on the fact that leaders have created a positive school climate in which staff feel as though they can take risks. As we all know, there are many issues to collaborative conversations, and we need not look any further than the Collaborative Leadership Framework to understand the different roles that play out in a collaborative group. However, understanding those roles can best help us understand how to inspire synergy among the group.

The bystanders merely sit quietly and will agree with the group, but we know who the bystanders are already in most cases. Can we reach out to them after the meeting to ask for their input? Is it possible they are reflective and need more time to think than the meeting allows? The regulators are often the group leaders who will tell group members what they need to do. Can we instead ask those people to be a timer or recording secretary of the group to help us stick to the agenda at hand? Negotiators may throw in an "I wonder if . . ." to get the group more aligned with them, but perhaps that is necessary so we can think about the questions they ask, which may help make our decision or solution much stronger. Finally, collaborators take in all of the ideas of the group and lay them out for the group to decide upon.

In schools, we have a group of adults that we are tasked to work with every day. We can either look at them as an obstacle to the solution, or we can use a strengths-based approach to have them help us every time. One of the best places to see these individuals in action is in our professional learning community (PLC) meetings or in our faculty meetings.

Stop. Collaborate and Listen!

Flipped Faculty Meeting

- Coconstruct goals with staff based on their current realities.
- Find one or two resources (e.g., YouTube videos, articles, blogs) that help model how to meet the goal.
- Send the resource out three days before the meeting with the expectation that participants watch or read it.
- In some cases, require staff to bring evidence of how they approached the topic (e.g., feedback, evidence-based observations, teaching strategies).
- Spend the first 20 minutes (time varies) of the faculty meeting discussing the topic to make sure everyone has a common understanding.
- At the meeting, participants get into groups of three or four (with people other than their friends) and share their examples.
- Groups share what they have learned from one another.

We should look at these individuals, as best we can, in a positive light as opposed to a negative one. Sure, some people seem to wake up in the morning and have the goal to block every decision that the principal has, while others may be resistant because they need to think through the issue before they can come to grips with it.

There are many ways to make sure everyone contributes to the group think tank so that teacher voice is respected and collective teacher efficacy is maximized. The following are roles that each member of the group can take. It is important to note that the larger the staff in a faculty meeting or whole-school setting, the more groups that will have to be established, which means consistency among the roles of each group is necessary.

Group Roles

Group Leader: For each collaborative inquiry that takes place, it's important to have a different leader each time. For example, if each faculty meeting results in some sort of collaborative inquiry question (Donohoo, 2016), it's important to change the roles so one person isn't always the leader. The group leader focuses on the intention of the collaboration and asks the questions to get to the appropriate answer. Those questions are often the old-school who, what, where, when, and why.

Note-Taker/Evidence Collector: It is highly important that a person has the job of taking notes to make sure that there is proper evidence for reflection. If no one writes notes, it is possible that participants will not remember exactly what was discussed. Often, note-takers cannot participate in the discussion because they have to listen carefully to the input of each member. This is another reason why it's important that the roles change for every collaborative conversation, because note-takers could easily find themselves in the bystander quadrant of the Collaborative Leadership Framework.

Timer: A timer is needed to make sure that the group is on time. However, the timer needs to also establish a protocol that states one person cannot dominate the whole conversation.

Critical Friend: It's really important that one person plays the role of devil's advocate—that is, there needs to be one person who looks at the obstacles to each suggestion that is given by the group. This is to make sure that the group looks at the problem and resolution from all sides.

Group Protocols

The group must also establish a protocol for learning from one another and understand they are responsible for action planning. One way to do this is to brainstorm resolutions.

Brainstorm resolutions: One of the things that our child study team (CST) did when I was a principal was write the suggestions on paper, the whiteboard, or Smart board, and then put the initials of the person responsible for following through on that suggestion next to it so that accountability was established. For example, if I suggested calling a parent, my initials would go next to that suggestion.

And to make sure their group was as effective as they thought it was when the collaboration was taking place, the group could do the following:

Videotape conversation: One of the other steps collaborative groups can take is to videotape the session (Knight, 2014). Members of the collaborative group can watch the videotape to see how they actually collaborated or if they dominated the conversation—or worse, didn't say anything at all.

Solving Issues: Collaboration in Action

The first part of a collaborative conversation is the problem at hand. What is the issue the group is trying to solve? We need to talk through difficult issues, but too often we wait until we are in them to discuss them, which is reactive rather than proactive. In order to effectively negotiate our way through difficult discussions, we should set parameters before the discussion. We would never ask students to engage in center-based learning or use Makerspaces without first teaching them how to do it. And yet, we often dive into the deep end of collaborative conversations without setting up some sort of parameters first.

Stop. Collaborate and Listen!

Possible Parameters for Collaborative Conversations

- What is the topic to be discussed?
- Everyone has two minutes to compose her or his thoughts.
- Establish that this is a safe space to express ideas.
- Gossiping after the meeting is not allowed. Just the facts should be shared.
- Everyone contributes.
- One person talks at a time.
- Everyone needs to back up opinions with evidence.
- People are allowed to ask clarification questions or make statements such as "What I am hearing you say is...."
- At the end of the meeting, reflect on what was said.
- Are action steps needed?
- Who is responsible for the steps?

As an example of the problem-solving process, Iowa high school principal J. R. Kuchs and his administrative team wrote about the process they went through to battle a morale issue. J. R. reached out to me through Voxer and asked for some suggestions to work through the morale issue, and I told him about what I did as a principal. He used the idea, and to say it had an impact would be an understatement.

Practitioner's Voice

Morale Is Low!

J. R. Kuchs, Principal
Building Leadership Team: Amy Lueders,
  Wes Golden, and Dan Pataska
Clinton High School
Clinton, Iowa

Our school, Clinton High, located on the Iowa side of the Mississippi River, has roughly 1,000 kids and 100 staff members. We have been identified as a Model PLC (professional learning community) school and also a Model RTI site (response to intervention) by Solution Tree. We hosted over 100 schools to share with them our systematic way to ensure that all students achieve at high levels. Not bad, right? What could possibly be wrong?

Plenty.

As the building principal, accessibility and positivity for me are key. Before the 2016–2017 school year, I moved my office from its previous isolated location to an office that is located on a main hallway, where not even a buffer of a secretary would be between me and everyone else. I thought this move, coupled with an "open-door" policy—all staff having my phone number, increasing hallway and classroom visibility, and helping anyone with any problem—would allow me to be a collaborative leader.

It wasn't enough. Not even close.

In mid-October, the good vibes from the beginning of the year were officially over. It was the end of the "honeymoon." Trusted teachers with whom I had great relationships weren't as talkative as before. The three-minute morning conversations in the hallways were met with, "Hey, I got to go, I'll talk to you later." I wouldn't say it was icy, nor cold, but it was definitely chilly. I reflected and couldn't understand why this might be happening. I mean, how could it? My office is literally right off the hallway! My administration team and I were doing everything we could think of to be available for staff.

But it was what we weren't doing that was the problem.

Although we might have had the best intentions, our words and actions didn't line up. In what one teacher called "street corner discussions," small groups of teachers were participating in discussions that centered around all of the things they felt were not being addressed or dealt with by our administrative team. Another veteran teacher shared with me that things weren't going well and that end-of-the-year "burnout" actually came by late September.

Battle lines were being drawn, frustration was growing, and I was oblivious to it. I have always tried to bridge the "us-versus-them" gap because if we were going to make CHS even better, I always believed *we* had to do it together. To say my feelings were hurt would be a vast understatement. It was more like asking out your high school crush and she says yes, but come to find out, she had her eyes on the

(Continued)

(Continued)

varsity quarterback—but you would do for now, until the quarterback was available!

However, with a high school staff of over 100, we knew that the negativity was spreading like a virus through the hallways and our biweekly professional development Wednesdays. We needed more than isolated conversations with individual teachers to find the cure. With the guidance of Peter DeWitt, my team and I constructed an activity that would allow all members of our staff to have their thoughts heard without fear of retribution from the administrative team.

The Big Idea

We broke the school down into different teams of four to five people and gave them butcher paper to come up with their top three "Morale Busters" and their top three "Morale Boosters." Once they identified those six items, all teachers were asked to head to the gym to put their papers up on the walls—negative papers on one side and positive papers on another. Teachers were given six stickers (three for positive and three for negative) to place on a topic that they felt was the most important for them. This process allowed all staff members to share their frustrations in a systematic and nonthreatening way.

We informed the staff a week before this "Morale Bust and Boost" activity took place and did it instead of our regular early-out PD. There was a weird feeling leading up to the day of the activity. The chilly conversations that had been happening were replaced with nervous smiles. There were times people walking past me would look at the ground. It was unsettling.

I had always had a good relationship with members of our staff, so I think they were nervous to share their thoughts with me because they know I'm sensitive. No matter the fate of the activity, our administration team knew that we had good people in the building.

The results of the activity were shocking.

There really wasn't an attack on our administrative team. The "Morale Busters" were systematic things that policies dictated action or inaction by members of our school:

1. RTI (the very thing we are on the map for)

2. Too many initiatives and too many things to do at PD time and for "homework"

3. Staff accountability

The "Morale Boosters" were things that I was very pleased to see:

1. We work with really good people.

2. We are willing to help each other.

3. We like Friday Jeans and Spirit Days.

What we as an administrative team found was that the simple act of opening ourselves up to honest, unabashed feedback was a powerful one. We took some actionable steps that showed the staff that we listened. We returned the autonomy of the classrooms back to the teachers. Staff shared that this was the first time in over 15 years that they had an opportunity to share their thoughts and feelings, and just this process alone allowed some of the weight to be lifted from their shoulders—it empowered them.

CHS was not transformed overnight to the land of unicorns and rainbows. However, there is a sense of reserved positivity and optimism for the staff that they didn't feel prior to this action. It will be important for the administrative team to consistently monitor and take the temperature of the staff because those hallways can get awfully chilly!

In order to do this properly, leaders need to establish goals with the group, understand the projected outcomes, and agree upon what success criteria is necessary. This was evident when J. R. addressed the issues happening in Clinton High School. By doing this, the group understood how they knew they were successful after the collaboration took place:

- They found a desired outcome.
- Each member received a part of what he or she wanted.

- Participants felt comfortable sharing their opinions and seeing their opinions reflected in the outcome
- They wanted to be a part of a collaborative group again.

In the End

Stakeholders who feel valued by the leader will take a more active role in collaborative thinking. We are living in complicated times, which all contribute to our school climates. I have heard many people, both friends and strangers, say before a dinner party that we cannot talk about politics or sexual orientation. I worry that is flawed thinking because those discussions open up our learning. The difficult issues are the very topics we should be discussing in our school so we can foster supportive school climates. As much as we should be putting students first, we know that our school climates will never be the supportive, nurturing environments they can be until the adults in the school learn how to effectively talk with one another.

In order to overcome the difficult issues, we must learn to talk about them, and that only happens when leaders establish an inclusive school climate for all stakeholders. As you read in the chapter, the Collaborative Leadership Framework is just as important for our collaborative groups as it is to describe our collaborative leaders. Building collective efficacy, which has a 1.57 effect size, is only done well when all members of the group feel that they can share their voice, which helps raise the self-efficacy (0.63) of each member. There are clearly many ways in which to do that. Some of those ways are flipping faculty meetings, establishing protocols for groups, and having a shared understanding of how the group will know they were successful after their collaboration is finished.

Over the next few chapters, I will illustrate how to help engage more students in your school climate, as well as engage more teachers. It seems to be harder to do these days, given the issues going on in the world and the increased use of social media, reality television, and gaming. I believe that collaborative leadership is a necessary component of a positive school climate, and a positive school climate is a necessary component to collaborative leadership.

ACTION STEPS

- Make school climate a priority.
- What is your current reality when it comes to school climate?
- Gather evidence.
  - Will you use student, parent, or teacher surveys?
  - Decide how you will address the findings of those surveys with stakeholders.

DISCUSSION QUESTIONS

- In what ways is school climate important to you?
- Have you established protocols for collaborative groups at school?
- Can you see the relationship between collaborative groups and school climate?
- What has been your best collaborative experience?

TRUDY AND TIM

- What is Trudy's school climate? What would you think is her current reality?
- What is the current reality of Tim's school climate? How can he make it stronger?

3

Climate Change

Raising Student Self-Efficacy

Sixth graders who are held to fourth-grade expectations will be great fifth graders when they are in seventh grade; the gap never closes.

—Douglas Fisher, Nancy Frey, and John Hattie

School seems different these days. Perhaps it's because I was a school principal during a time when we had to practice "active-shooter drills"; or because I remember Columbine when I was a teacher; or because I remember sitting in my office, staring numbly at Twitter, when the Sandy Hook massacre took place. We live in a time of terrorist bombings in public places around the world and senseless shootings at schools. All of this weighs heavily on our school climates because this feeling of unsafety has been pervasive. We know that self-efficacy is *the confidence or strength of belief that we have in ourselves that we can make our learning happen,* but imagine how hard it is for students to feel a positive sense of efficacy when everything in their lives seems to be happening *to* them instead of happening *with* them.

When I was a kid growing up on Pinewood Road in Queensbury, New York, I was always outside. I didn't walk three miles uphill to school each way, but my mom did make us go outside every day, regardless of how cold the weather was. On weekends, I would go over to my best friend Todd's house, and we would head into the trails and play all day. I walked home alone and never worried about being abducted.

As a teacher, I began to notice that our students didn't play outside as much as we did when we were kids, and then when I was a principal in a town that looked a lot like the safe one I grew up in, parents would tell me that their children were not allowed to play outside unless they were supervised. It seems as though more and more students are spending more time in their virtual worlds than in their real world. Through research, we know that spending too much time indoors as opposed to outdoor play is detrimental to the social-emotional health of our students (Wells & Evans, 2003).

To make matters worse, because of increased accountability and mandates along with the stress of performing well on state standardized tests, schools around the country are cancelling recess in order to increase class time.

As you can imagine, taking away recess to increase class time—and the increased amount of sitting that will come along with it—will have a harmful impact on the school climate. It certainly doesn't raise the self-efficacy of the children within that school. Our students need brain breaks, regardless of whether they are in elementary, middle, or high school. This lack of exercise and movement leads to higher obesity rates in our students, which has a negative impact on student achievement (Gable, Krull, & Chang, 2012).

In fact, our children living in poverty are less likely to be able to go outside and play at home, so recess during the school day may offer them their only opportunity to play. The lack of recess and opportunity to play mixed with unhealthy diets leads to higher rates of obesity as well. In a national survey of more than 40,000 children, the Food Research and Action Center found that "obesity rates increased by 10 percent for all U.S. children 10 to 17 years old between 2003 and 2007, but by 23 percent during the same time period for low-income children" (Singh et al., 2010).

When I was an adjunct professor in the Graduate School of Education at the College of Saint Rose, I gave an assignment to help students better understand the communities where their students resided. The project required them to go to a grocery store in both the poorest and wealthiest sections of Albany, New York. Besides the high-end boutique markets, in the wealthiest section they also found grocery stories filled with the best produce. When they ventured over the poorest section of Albany to go through the grocery store, they couldn't find the produce and certainly didn't see any boutique markets. Why? The poorest section of Albany doesn't even have a grocery store. The nearest store was a bus ride or car ride to another part of the city. The only food immediately available to them was in fast-food restaurants or convenience stores.

Recess, obesity, gun violence, increased accountability, and mandates are topics in which the outside world and the school world collide, and they lead to lower levels of self-efficacy, which means lower student growth and achievement. This is probably not the most uplifting way to begin a chapter, but it does illustrate the reality that schools face—and the constant pressure collaborative leaders face. There are countless obstacles to raising the self-efficacy of our students, and student self-efficacy is directly related to achievement (Margolis & McCabe, 2003).

Social-Emotional Learning

There is no better time than the present to focus on school climate because the social-emotional health of our students is at risk, which is why social-emotional learning (SEL) is key to building that positive and inclusive school climate. The Collaborative for Academic, Social, and Emotional Learning (CASEL) defines social-emotional learning as

> the processes through which children and adults acquire and effectively apply the knowledge, attitudes and skills necessary to understand and manage emotions, set and achieve positive goals, feel and show empathy for others, establish and maintain positive relationships, and make responsible decisions. (2017, para. 1)

SEL is instrumental in increasing students' level of self-efficacy and inspiring them to take control over their own learning. In a meta-analysis involving more than 200 studies and 270,000 students, Durlak, Weissberg, Dymnicki, Taylor, and Schellinger (2011) found "those who participated in evidence-based SEL programs showed an 11 percentile-point gain in academic achievement compared to students who did not participate in SEL programs" (p. 1). Durlak and colleagues also found that the most successful SEL programs were those taught by classroom teachers or school personnel, and they "included assessments of social-cognitive and affective competencies that SEL programs targeted such as emotions recognition, stress-management, empathy, problem-solving, or decision-making skills" (2011, p. 13).

To make it easier for students to understand and develop self-efficacy, CASEL lists the following SEL competencies:

- **Self-awareness:** The understanding of one's emotions
- **Self-management:** Being able to regulate one's emotions, setting goals, and understanding how to reach those goals even during times of stress
- **Social awareness:** The ability to empathize with others

- **Relationship skills:** The ability to surround one's self with healthy and positive relationships, and how to help others in need
- **Responsible decision-making:** The ability to make positive choices for oneself

Unfortunately, only three states in the United States had comprehensive K–12 SEL standards with benchmarks by the end of 2015. However, by the end of 2016, 26 states had begun the process of joining the CASEL collaborative (Blad, 2016). This is a sign that SEL is on the upswing, and the competencies, or learner dispositions, could be a great way to start the process.

Learner dispositions are the dispositions students need to be self-confident learners. Collaborative leaders and teachers could take the CASEL competencies and use those as learner dispositions to focus on with staff, parents, and students. Those dispositions could help everyone understand the language of learning (Hattie, 2015b) and could be used as common language around the school community.

During a recent visit to the Bellingham (Massachusetts) Public Schools, where I have been working with leadership teams on the Collaborative Leadership Framework, South Elementary School behavior specialist Leslie Paterson showed me the many ways they are including the CASEL framework in their SEL curriculum. The dispositions are on display in the hallway and most classrooms and teachers are using them in their conversations with their students. Additionally, South Elementary School is working toward getting all of the teachers to use the CASEL words as part of their common language with students to help them increase their level of self-efficacy.

Imagine if all students, staff, parents, and leaders had consistent dialogue regarding self-awareness, self-management, social awareness, relationships skills, and responsible decision-making? Our school climates would improve, and perhaps—just perhaps—we would have fewer of these tragic events taking place.

Stop. Collaborate and Listen!

Learner Dispositions

- As a school building/district, create learning dispositions focused on SEL.
  - Those dispositions could be self-awareness, self-management, social awareness, relationships skills, self-efficacy, and responsible decision-making.
- Create an SEL school team that includes a school counselor, teachers, administrator, nurse, parents, and students.
  - Meet after school once a month to create schoolwide activities that can be easily used by staff (e.g., a poster, writing, or social media contest).
  - As a school principal I went on our school news every Friday and once a month and asked students to participate in a creative writing contest around one central idea, and hung the writing pieces on the main office wall for the month. Incorporate social media, and choose a couple of the pieces of student writing to post as a blog on the school website.

Minoritized Populations

Leaders and teachers have to be concerned with all students when it comes to SEL, but one of the groups that often get left out of the school climate discussion is that of our minoritized populations. In order to create a school climate that is supportive and inclusive, we have to address some of the biggest issues we face, which also happen to be the issues many of us avoid talking about. In Chapter 2, I provided a vignette about how avoiding tough conversations limits our learning, and one of the tough conversations is when we talk about our minoritized populations. Harper (2012) explains the use of the word *minoritized* instead of *minority*:

> Persons are not born into a minority status nor are they minoritized in every social context (e.g., their families,

racially homogeneous friendship groups, or places of worship). Instead, they are rendered minorities in particular situations and institutional environments that sustain an overrepresentation of Whiteness. (p. 9)

Of Te Kotahitanga, the program that was produced from their seminal work with Maori high school students in New Zealand, Russell Bishop and Mere Berryman write,

We were told time and time again by many of the interview participants that negative, deficit thinking on the part of teachers was fundamental to the development of negative relations and interactions between the students and their teachers, resulting in frustration and anger for all concerned. (2009, p. 1)

As you can imagine, deficit thinking is not confined to just Maori students in New Zealand. Deficit thinking is one of the reasons why I created the Meet, Model, and Motivate framework for the collaborative leadership work.

No matter what country we are in or whether we are teaching and leading at the primary, middle, or high school level, we are surrounded by individuals who have deficit thinking. In my own work on safeguarding LGBT students (DeWitt, 2012), I found that the leaders and teachers who were not engaging LGBT students either lacked an understanding of the population and therefore didn't use the common language (such as the LGBT acronym), or they had deficit thinking about the population (which is why I began this section by explaining the difference between *minority* and *minoritized*). LGBT students are minoritized in many schools around North America, the United Kingdom, and Australia. This process of being minoritized also happens to Native American, African American, and many other nonwhite students in North America; Aboriginal students in Australia; Maori and Pacific Island students in New Zealand; and many other populations around the world.

If we are to effectively create a school climate, we should follow the important work of Russell Bishop and Mere Berryman. Although Bishop and Berryman created Te Kotahitanga for Maori students in New Zealand, I believe the work offers many lessons schools can learn when it comes to minoritized populations. It begins by creating an effective teacher profile, which was initially "constructed from reflecting upon the numerous conversations we had with the students, their whānau, their principals and their teachers when we were constructing the narratives of experience" (Bishop & Berryman, 2006, p. 1). Bishop and Berryman went on to write,

> The narratives are used to allow teachers to critically reflect upon and compare their own understandings about how Māori students see the world and experience schooling with how Māori students themselves experience schooling. This reflection is a necessary part of the consideration by teachers of the part they play in their students' learning. (p. 1)

Throughout this book and in others I have written, I have expressed the importance of dialogue—and ways to go about it—with minoritized and nonminoritized students. If teachers and leaders care for all of the students that enter their buildings on a daily basis, we need to keep the dialogue open and consider how our biases obstruct us from engaging more students.

Bishop and Berryman go on to highlight five relationships and interactions that can be seen in an effective teacher's classroom. Although the five relationships and interactions are Maori words, leaders and teachers looking for ways to increase the self-efficacy of students and create a supportive school climate will understand how they can be developed in their schools, regardless of the minoritized population. They are as follows:

- **Manaakitanga:** Caring for students as Māori
- **Mana Motuhake:** Caring for the performance of Māori students

- **Ngā Whakapiringatanga:** Creating a secure, well-managed learning environment
- **Wānanga:** Engaging in effective learning interactions with Māori students
- **Kotahitanga:** Using student progress to inform future teaching practices (2010, pp. 58–59)

All of the information provided in this section leads to a tool that I hope leaders and teachers will find useful because it will lead to deeper conversations among educators, students, and families and will help aid teachers in finding more effective methods to engage students. It's called the Early Warning System.

The Early Warning System (EWS)

School climate and SEL require us to understand which students are at risk of crashing and burning while they are in our care. It is our job as educators to increase the self-efficacy of every student that comes to our school. Sadly, we know that the idea of raising the self-efficacy of each student is complicated because some students come to us with far more issues than we ever experienced in our lives. They come with red flags.

Red flags—we have all heard that term before. A red flag indicates when we are at risk of being ineffective. Our students are surrounded by potential red flags. Teachers talk about them and they show up in our data conversations when a student isn't being successful, and we start talking about their home life or their absenteeism or tardiness from school.

My partner Douglas is a director at the New York State Department of Health. Many years ago, he created an Early Warning System (EWS) for the nonprofit organizations he worked with in New York State. He started seeing the same red flags that indicated the nonprofit AIDS organizations he worked with were at risk of fiscal issues that would affect the organizations' financial health and ultimately their program services. There were items such as whether their expenses exceeded their revenue each year, a negative net assets balance (net worth of the agency), a bad debt-to-equity ratio, or an unfavorable audit opinion by their independent auditor, all of which were red flags of poor fiscal health. Yes, very financial stuff; however, as we spoke more and more about this system, we wondered if there could be a similar early warning system for our students. While we may be looking at many of the red flags or indicators, we lack having a system in place to allow us to be proactive rather than reactive.

Before I dive into different elements that should or could be on a school's early warning system checklist, I want to write about the challenges of creating one in the first place. We need to make sure that we find a balance between knowing when our students are at risk and putting them at risk because of our expectations for them. As school leaders, we need to remember to meet people where they actually are, and not where our biases lead us to believe they may be. After we engage them, we need to model what it is we hope to see in their learning and then motivate them to try it on their own. It's deeply rooted in this idea of self-efficacy because it is all about helping them increase their self-efficacy.

To be clear, we do not lower our expectations of students because they end up red flagged in our early warning system. The EWS is supposed to highlight which students are at risk, but it means that we have to maintain high expectations for them at the same time we empathize with their situations and help find resources for them to better meet their needs.

Early Warning System Indicators

There are many indicators that can appear on a school's EWS. I will provide some here; however, leaders should value the voices of their community and may come up with their own. All indicators should be measurable.

Early Warning System Indicators

Attendance

Many students suffer from *chronic absenteeism*, defined as missing 10 percent or more of their school days in a year, but very few schools keep track of this issue. Chronic absenteeism is associated with lower academic performance.

Possible Solutions

- Offer incentives for students who show up to school on a daily basis.
- Create attendance task forces; they can create campaigns to help parents understand the importance of attendance.
- Offer mentoring to students who are chronically absent, meaning that they have a yearlong mentor who helps engage them in coming to school by setting personal goals.

High-Stakes Assessments

K–8 state tests: Clearly, using state testing for the EWS is going to be controversial. The fact is that there is research supporting, refuting, and anywhere in the middle, the topic. But with some changes and innovation, test scores can be used to help students succeed. For example, if test scores were made available within a matter of weeks, school leadership teams would be able to use them to inform instruction for the remainder of the academic year. If students are flagged as being nonproficient, instructional leaders can intervene in a timely manner to give those students the support they need to improve.

High school standardized tests: Across the United States, states use a variety of tests. For example, New York State has the regents exams, Massachusetts has the Massachusetts Comprehensive Assessment System (MCAS), and Texas has the State of Texas Assessment of Academic Readiness (STAAR). Depending on the state of the school community, these can be used in the EWS process.

(Continued)

(Continued)

International Note: International tests vary throughout the world. Finland has one high-stakes test that students take as an exit exam out of high school, while Japan has one high-stakes test to get into high school and one to get out. Most universities in those countries have an entrance exam as well. However, Australia has the National Assessment Program Literacy and Numeracy (NAPLAN), which is an annual national assessment for all students in Years 3, 5, 7, and 9. Schools receive the results, which can be used as part of the EWS. England, Wales, New Zealand, and Denmark all have national tests as well. Denmark's national test is a computer adaptive test (CAT) and is used only to guide instruction, so it is not made public (Wandall, 2011).

Curriculum-Based Measures (CBM)

We have to look at our locally developed measures to make sure that those tests are providing us with the information we need to help guide our instruction. Fuchs, Deno, and Mirkin (1984) found that "along with better student achievement and pedagogy, students were more knowledgeable about their own learning as a result of the systematic measurement and evaluation treatment" (p. 458) when teachers used curriculum-based measures.

Clarke writes (2009) the following:

> Nearly 30 years of empirical evidence tells us that CBM provides a valid and reliable indicator of student progress in basic academic areas, especially reading, math, and writing, and that it can have a positive impact on student achievement. . . . In contrast to standardized achievement tests, which do not provide immediate feedback, CBM tests are given frequently to track student progress toward annual goals, monitor the effectiveness of interventions, and make instructional changes as needed throughout the year. (p. 30)

Although CBMs are beneficial, it is important to remember that teachers need to be trained how to give them. The discussion of the results for each student is one of the main reasons why they can help teachers guide instruction and help increase the self-efficacy of students.

Free/Reduced Lunch

Harwell and LeBeau (2010) found that "free lunch eligibility is a poor measure of socioeconomic status." However, Bartik (2013) found that "the average test score differential between free/reduced lunch (FRL) students, and non FRL students, in both reading and math across different grades is about seven tenths or 70 percent of one standard deviation." Bartik further explains that statistic by writing that "25 percent of students ineligible for lunch subsidies would score worse than the average free and reduced price lunch student, but 75 percent would score better than the average free and reduced price lunch student." In other words, although free/reduced lunch may be a poor indicator of poverty, it is a worthy indicator of achievement.

For the purposes of the EWS, teachers and leaders need to know if particular students are eligible for FRL and whether they get it or whether they are eligible and don't have the paperwork completed to get FRL. I know that sounds simple, but as a principal, I had many students who were eligible for FRL but their parents had not completed the necessary paperwork.

Teacher–Student Engagement

I need to be up-front and say that this indicator will be more difficult because it is easy for us to look at attendance, test scores, and family engagement, but it's more difficult for us to be honestly reflective with evidence to understand whether our teaching is truly engaging our students. This is why I saved this indicator for last.

To be fully honest, this may have to be one of the indicators we need to look at first. We need to know if students are struggling because they don't understand the concept due to a gap in learning or whether they don't understand the concept because of bad teaching. It's easier to change the child than it is to change the child's environment.

We need to understand whether our teaching is really engaging and whether students are being taught relevant content. In a 2015 Gallup poll that surveyed over 900,000 students, only 23 percent of students said "they get to do what they do best every day," 43 percent answered that "in the last seven days, I have learned something interesting at school,"

(Continued)

(Continued)

and only 39 percent "believed the adults in school cared about them" (Gallup, 2016).

Out of all the indicators, we should be most passionate about this one because this is the one we control. If the teacher's strategies are not engaging, the student does not appear on the EWS because we as leaders need to work with the teacher on increasing student engagement. However, if we have changed our strategies, brainstormed new strategies with colleagues or our child study team, and tried to find ways to engage students through goal setting and incentives and the student is still not engaged, this indicator needs to be highlighted.

To help teachers and leaders create classroom climates as well as a school climate that focuses on learning, the following pages will provide some of Hattie's (2012b) high-impact strategies to help increase student engagement. Each one of these strategies requires a great deal of thought, conversation among peers, and preparation before it will reach its full impact.

High-Impact Strategies

Assessment-Capable Learners (1.44)

When workshop participants see the 1.44 effect size, they typically ask if it's possible to get three years' worth of growth out of students in one year. The simple answer is yes. The difficult part of all of this is how to teach students to be self-directed learners, and unfortunately, it's because of us that they may not be doing it. When we easily give them the answer because they pause too long to think about it, or we don't provide them with learning intentions and success criteria (how will they know they are successful when they complete the assignment?), we are taking away the opportunity for students to engage in their own learning.

Our school and classroom climates need to be places where students can take risks, and they take risks by being allowed to learn from error. Additionally, we need to make sure that students have the opportunity to approach problems in different ways, and they should be allowed to ask questions of their teacher when going through the problem. Students should be asking as many questions of us as we are asking of them, which means there needs to be increased dialogue in the classroom, and that happens when students see their learning as relevant. Just like teachers who don't like professional development being done to them, there are many students who don't like schooling being done to them. Learning is a two-way street and involves multiple avenues on both sides of that two-way street. The bottom line is that students need to know the learning intentions and success criteria, and they need to find their learning relevant and inspiring.

Classroom Discussion (0.82)

Classroom discussion is powerful when done correctly. For this learning influence to be powerful and reach the effect size attached to it, it's important to understand that students need the learning intentions and success criteria. Do you see a pattern yet? Without the learning intentions and success criteria, students won't know what to discuss. And in order to engage in a high-impact class discussion, students need to understand the protocol for the discussion. It cannot be a free-for-all, so protocols are important.

Feedback (0.75)

Hattie's research shows us that there are three types of feedback we give and get during learning. Those three types are task (new learning), process (some degree of proficiency), and self-regulation (high degree of proficiency). The other thing to remember is that as important as it is to give feedback, it's important to understand how to take it. In *Thanks for the Feedback*, Stone and Heen (2015) reported that people want three types of feedback: appreciation (tell me how good I am), coaching (here's a better way to do it), and evaluative (here's where you stand). And yes,

(Continued)

(Continued)

learning intentions and success criteria are key in the process of providing and receiving effective feedback.

There are many other high-impact strategies that teachers and leaders can use, but I will end with metacognitive strategies.

Metacognitive Strategies (0.69)

There are two types of metacognition to understand. Darling-Hammond and colleagues (2003) have researched reflection, or thinking about what we know, and self-regulation, which is managing how we go about learning. Clearly, these two types of metacognition take a lot of front loading on the part of the teacher, which means providing students with a common understanding of concepts before they dive into practicing them.

There are numerous examples of metacognitive activities that teachers can do with students, and the following are just a few of them:

Fish Bowl: Select a group of four students and provide them with a problem to solve while the rest of the class sits around them and listens to their method of solving the issue. Those in the inner group are allowed to leave at any time, which means that one person from the outer circle can jump in at any time.

3, 2, 1 Exit Tickets: At the end of a class, students are asked to take a ticket on which they write down three things they learned, two things they are hoping to learn more about, and one thing they will hold on to long after the class is over. There are variations of this practice, and I have even seen teachers do entrance tickets.

Entrance Tickets: I learned about this from some teachers in Bellingham, Massachusetts. They begin class by asking students to write down one or two things they hope to learn about a topic (given their understanding of the topic after they left the last class). The teachers use that as their formative assessment while teaching the material.

Other more popular metacognitive activities are Think-Pair-Share, reflection journals, learning maps, and those listed in Figure 3.1.

Figure 3.1   High-Impact Strategies for Students

Student expectations (assessment capable learners)	1.44
Response to intervention	1.07
Classroom discussion	0.82
Feedback	0.75
Evaluation and reflection (with evidence)	0.75
Reciprocal teaching	0.74
Metacognitive strategies	0.69
Self-questioning	0.64
Study skills	0.63
Concept mapping	0.60
Direct instruction	0.59
Peer tutoring	0.55
Cooperative versus competitive learning	0.54
Goals	0.50

Source: Adapted from Hattie (2015a).

The last few sections of the EWS are somewhat out of the control of teachers and leaders, but Hattie's research has shown that these indicators have an enormous impact on student success. The last three indicators are retention, mobility, and family engagement. Retention is one indicator that seems to be in the hands of the student's current teacher, but that is not always the case. The student's present teacher may not have any control over the fact that a student had been retained prior to entering their classroom.

Additionally, all three have an impact on the self-efficacy of the learner, as well as the school climate. A student who has been retained, lacks family engagement, and has moved frequently will feel different about the school community than students who have not experienced those issues.

Additional Early Warning System Indicators

Retention (–0.13)

As you can see from the effect size associated with retention, it shows a profound negative effect on student growth and achievement. This plays an important part in the Early Warning System (EWS) because teachers and leaders need to know who has been retained in the past because they are at risk of being retained again. West (2012) found that retention is a very complicated issue because the reasons why students are retained differ among school districts, states, and state policies concerning grade-level exit exams. What the research shows us is that students who were retained are at risk of dropping out of school if they are retained a second time. Therefore, it's important to understand which of our students were retained, whether they have received high-quality supports since their retention, and teachers understand how their present achievement and growth is in their academic setting. On the EWS, students who are retained are given a *Y* for Yes, and those students who were not retained are simply provided with an *N* for no.

Mobility (–0.34)

Out of all of Hattie's (2015d) research, mobility has by far the most negative impact on student learning. The United States Government Accountability Office (USGAO, 2010) found that "students who change schools the most frequently (four or more times) represented about 13 percent of all kindergarten through eighth grade (K–8)" (p. 3). The USGAO went on to report that these students who were transient were "disproportionately poor, African American, and from families that didn't own their home. About 11.5 percent of schools also had high rates of mobility—more than 10 percent of K–8 students left by the end of the school year" (p. 9).

Given this definition of a transient student, you may not label some students *transient* as you thought you might. Using the scale of changing schools four times between kindergarten and eighth grade, on the

EWS teachers and leaders would mark *Y* for yes and *N* for no, but they may also want to calculate how many schools the students did move from and to. Some of the better news where transient students are concerned is that Hattie's research found that students who found a friend within the first two weeks to a month of school were less likely to be impacted negatively by the move than students who did not maintain any friendships at all.

Family Engagement (0.51)

Students who have involved parents are more likely to be successful in school. Parental engagement has a 0.51 effect size, which is well over the 0.40 that represents a year's worth of growth for a year's input. These days, more and more schools are beginning to call it *family engagement* because we know the family structure has changed, and our language needs to change to fit the changing structure. Family engagement is a necessary component to the EWS because if students who have involved parents do better in school, then students without engaged families are at risk of struggling or failing in school. Just because a family isn't engaged in their child's schooling doesn't mean that child is doomed to fail, but it is more likely that those children without home support will struggle.

Possible Solutions

- Create a strong home–school family partnership, which is something I will explain more in Chapter 5.
- Let parents in on the secret of school. Create conversations to help them understand the language of learning, which means they can understand what learning is all about in our 21st century world. This is not to be confused with using educational jargon or acronyms such as NCLB, AIS, or ESSA. It means talking with parents about what good learning looks like, which means that teachers, leaders, students, and staff have to understand what good learning looks like as well. I have already mentioned using the CASEL competencies, which can also be used to develop a language of learning.

Using the Early Warning System

First and foremost, we have to make the EWS as easy as possible for teachers because they will ultimately be the ones filling it out two times a year. The indicators previously mentioned could be on an Excel spreadsheet. However, the conversation around each indicator is what is important. How do we go about providing time? The following are possible ways to provide teachers with time to go through the EWS process:

- Release time (half or full days) to go through the process
- Prep time
- PLC discussions
- After school
- Allow two weeks to go through the process for each student
- For teachers with large caseloads (e.g., high school, middle school, and junior high school teachers), the homeroom teacher takes over the EWS process.

The reason why the discussion needs to take place is that the teacher–student engagement indicator may involve a simple yes or no, but we know the discussion is the important part. Teachers may believe they are doing everything possible to engage the student in need, but they may be missing one strategy that could help, which a critical friend could help them with during the discussion. Remember that this book focuses on collaboration, so teachers should not engage in this process alone. Out of the seven indicators, most students will appear on each one. If a student doesn't appear on any, the teachers should be wondering if they are engaging those students to the extent that they could be. However, when a student appears on four or more indicators, we know that there is an issue and they are red flagged. Remember that we are not tracking students but using the information we have in real time to find ways to help meet their needs. As I have written before, do we go to SEL resources to help those students being red flagged, or do we need to check out Tomlinson's work on differentiated instruction or Hattie's work in high-impact strategies or explore the idea of universal design for learning (UDL)? Collaborative leaders provide the resources teachers need during and after they go through this process.

Two times a year, teachers should engage in the EWS process. They should take the information they have and plot which students are in which category because the plotting will enable them to come up with common themes, making it easier to address the issues. For example, four or five students may appear on the parent involvement indicator, which means the teacher can make a targeted effort to get the parents involved by making positive phone calls home. Positive phone calls are always the best way to get the conversation started. Other times, there may be a number of students in the teacher–student engagement indicator, which means the teacher can work with a critical friend on high-impact strategies.

Early Warning System Process

- Teachers work in groups (grade level, department, or homeroom).
- Considering they have all of the evidence collected, they go through the EWS process for each student.
- After the process is completed for all students, teachers plot their information by common indicators. How many students are red flagged by each indicator?
- What action steps can be taken for each indicator?
  - Positive phone calls home
  - Student interest inventories
  - Learning intentions and success criteria
  - Goal setting

As a school or school district initiates this process, they may find that using a whole school database is more helpful. When students appear on five or more of the indicators, they should be looking at the interventions that need to be used. Remember—and I need to say this several times—this document is used not to track students but to help teachers and leaders understand who is most at risk. Tracking students is "ranking students based on their perceived intellectual abilities," which "results in different access to academic curriculum and the opportunity to learn" (Burris, 2014, p. 3). We shouldn't lower our expectations because a student appears on five of the indicators, but we should adjust our strategies that we are using with them.

A Warning About the EWS

We need to make sure that we find a balance between knowing when our students are at risk and putting them at risk because of our expectations for them. Given what we read about Tim Cooper in the introduction, we know he may approach the Early Warning System in a holistic way to assemble his instructional leadership team to brainstorm different resources for each student who is red flagged. In Trudy's case, she may potentially do the same or she may have a knee-jerk reaction in which the students end up with special services they don't need in order to get them prepared for a standardized test they may or may not pass. In that moment when Tim and Trudy each decide what to do, we either chip away at a positive school climate or help students feel that we care about them.

The EWS is supposed to highlight which students are at risk, but it means that we have to maintain high expectations for them at the same time we empathize with their situations and help find resources for them to better meet their needs. The bottom line is that just because we have students on the EWS doesn't mean they are worthy of our lowering our expectations for them. The EWS is supposed to help us understand how to better meet their needs. We are always at risk of lowering our expectations.

In the End

Our students should be given a fair shot to be successful in school. It's our job to help all students exceed their own expectations. We live in a world that seems to focus on the negative, and we have our fair share of tragic issues to deal with in school and in our outside worlds. With this feeling of heaviness that is taking place, we need to work on the social-emotional learning (SEL) of our students and ourselves, which I will dive into in a later chapter. However, we also have to look at the pressures we are applying to students and whether or not some of our policies and rules are adding to the pressure our students are feeling. Taking away recess and adding more instructional time only leads to burnout and harms the SEL of our students and our teachers.

The Early Warning System (EWS) is a tool I hope leaders and teachers will use to lead to better discussions about the supports we have in place for our students most at risk. Schools have access to so much data but hardly use it. It is my hope that the EWS allows teachers and leaders to bring their evidence to the table and have deep discussions about all of their students. All of these discussions, whether they are academic or focus on SEL, will help lead to building the self-efficacy of students, which will in turn lead to building the collective efficacy of the school community.

As I close out this chapter on student self-efficacy and move on to the efficacy of teachers, I feel it is important to give leaders and teachers a takeaway. If we want our school climates to be places where students can raise their own self-efficacy and become self-directed learners, we need to look at the surface- and deep-level learning that is taking place in all of our classrooms.

What Are the Best Strategies for Surface-to-Deep Learning?

Peter DeWitt (2016c)

April 21, 2016
Finding Common Ground Blog—blogs.edweek.org

If it's done correctly, teaching is both rewarding and complicated. The rewarding part is when we see students achieve or overcome some new learning, whether that's social-emotional or academic. In these days of social media, teaching is rewarding because we get to see students whom we had in our classrooms long ago grow up and find a passion in their choice of career.

However, teaching is also complicated because it's not just about teaching students "stuff." Teaching is about using a variety of strategies to help students learn information they need for the future, and it's about teaching students how to ask questions in order to have some level of control over their own learning, so they find a love for learning.

To the outside perspective, teaching may look like we all open up a textbook and teach the next concept that comes on the next page, as students sit at their desks waiting for us to tell them what that concept may be and how they can use it. Perhaps in some classrooms—or far too many classrooms—that may be how teaching actually is for the students sitting in the classroom.

However, in other classrooms, teaching and learning seem to come together fluently, although there is a lot of planning that took place ahead of time. Teachers ask questions but don't dominate the talk in the classrooms, and students ask questions back to the teacher or in partnership groups with peers. Additionally, they use different strategies to acquire the learning—like problem-based learning as well as personalization—to help increase the engagement and go from surface to deep.

This is important for teachers, school leaders, and instructional coaches to understand because when we all come together to talk about learning in our schools (i.e., faculty meetings, teacher observations, walkthroughs), we should spend part of that time focusing on how to get students from surface-level learning to a deeper level and then ultimately get them to the place where they transfer that learning—which may become their passion when we meet them later on Facebook and Instagram.

It all begins with learning intentions and success criteria. This can be controversial for teachers because success criteria means showing students what success looks like before they complete a learning task in the classroom. This should not be so controversial. Imagine sending a child into a soccer game without his or her ever having watched a soccer match on television or in real life.

We would never do that.

John Hattie and Gregory Donoghue (2016) write this about students knowing the success criteria:

> A prediction from the model of learning is that when students learn how to gain an overall picture of what is to be learnt, have an understanding of the success criteria for the lessons to come and are somewhat clear at the outset about what it means to master the lessons, then their subsequent learning is maximized. The overall effect across the 31 meta-analyses is 0.54, with the greatest effects relating to providing students with success criteria, planning and prediction, having intentions to implement goals, setting standards for self-judgements and the difficulty of goals. (p. 6)

When students know the learning intentions and success criteria, they can go from surface level to deep and even transfer learning better than they could if they never had it before. After teachers use learning intentions and success criteria, they can move on to different strategies that will lead to each level of learning.

Hattie and Donoghue (2016) focus on acquiring and consolidating the different levels of learning. When teachers work with students on acquiring surface-level learning, they are teaching students to use strategies such as *highlighting, note-taking, mnemonics, underlining,* and *imagery.* When students go to the next level of consolidating surface-level learning,

(Continued)

(Continued)

they are using strategies such as *test taking, rehearsal,* and *learning how to receive feedback.*

The authors go on to focus on acquiring deep-level learning and suggest strategies such as *organization, strategy monitoring, concept mapping,* and *metacognitive strategies.* The next step is to consolidate that deep learning by using strategies such as *self-questioning (i.e., metacognitive strategies), self-monitoring, self-explanation, self-verbalizing (i.e., internal dialogue of the learner is made verbal), peer tutoring, collaboration,* and *critical-thinking techniques (e.g., inquiry, questioning).*

Teaching students these strategies, and how to use them, will all help lead to transfer learning, which is the ultimate goal for us as teachers. This, of course, takes us back to the success criteria we used to start all of this in the first place. Hattie and Donoghue (2016) write,

> If the success criteria is the retention of accurate detail (surface learning), then lower-level learning strategies will be more effective than higher-level strategies. However, if the intention is to help students understand context (deeper learning) with a view to applying it in a new context (transfer), then higher level strategies are also needed. (p. 4)

In the End

Why does all of this matter? We often throw students into deep-learning situations without providing them with surface-level learning first, nor do we provide the strategies needed when they come to a point that is very challenging.

Talking about surface-level, deep-level, and transfer learning, as well as the strategies to use at each point and the questions to ask, will help strengthen the learning that happens in the classroom and can ultimately lead to a higher level of student engagement.

Imagine having the time in our PLCs or faculty meetings to explore topics such as questioning and learning strategies instead of spending our time solely on pacing, testing, or random adult issues where we complain about a lack of student engagement instead of focusing on the questions we ask that may actually increase student engagement.

ACTION STEPS

- Make sure students get recess at the elementary and middle level.
- Understand the importance of brain breaks for all students K–12.
- Take a look at your SEL curriculum. Do you have it? Are teachers using it?
- Create an Early Warning System (EWS).
- Gather evidence to help you in the EWS process:
  - Attendance
  - State tests
  - Locally developed growth measures
  - Free/reduced lunch
  - Attendance
  - Retention
  - Mobility
  - Teacher–student engagement

DISCUSSION QUESTIONS

- What does SEL mean to you?
- What part does SEL play in your school community?
- What are some issues you face that SEL might help alleviate?
- How would you use the EWS?
- Besides the indicators provided in this chapter, what indicators would you add?
- Why is it so important to understand the issue of tracking as you put together your EWS?

TIM AND TRUDY

- How might Tim and Trudy use the EWS differently?
- Are there indicators they would both use?
- What indicators might each one value differently?

4

Increasing
Teacher
Self-Efficacy

*For positive changes to occur in schools, everyone and anyone
who is truly committed to making a difference must listen to
students and teachers.*

—Russ Quaglia and Lisa Lande

I f we want schools to improve and become places that
engage more students in the relevant learning they need,
then we need to look at the quality of teaching within schools.
This means we have to focus on issues such as the self-
efficacy of teachers and the individual classroom climates that
students walk into every day. This is not to set up a one-sided
conversation that schools are failing and teachers are sub-par,
because it's not. The reality is that there are countless great
teachers who engage students every day, despite the fact their
schools may not have the supplies they need or the obstacles
the students face from homes that they come from or the social-
emotional issues that they have experienced because of tragic
situations. These teachers create safe and engaging classrooms

where students are inspired to ask questions as much as they answer them and learn to work collaboratively with others.

The quality of teaching is the most important in-school factor that contributes to learning and achievement (Fullan & Hargreaves, 2016). Leadership is about finding improved methods to enhance the learning that all stakeholders engage in, which is central to a collaborative school climate. Those improved methods begin with research and feedback. Fullan and Hargreaves believe that "the essence of system success is a culture of daily interaction, engaging pedagogy, mutual trust, and development. And regular, quality feedback related to improvement" (2016, p. 8).

The Cycle of Collaborative Teacher Observation: A Review

In *Collaborative Leadership: Six Influences That Matter Most* (2016a), I focused on the observation process that leaders and teachers can go through together. The key word in that statement is *together*. Effective teacher observation should be a partnership between the leader and teacher involved. For too long, teachers have felt as though observations were done to them, and they were often left without any quality feedback to help them improve. This type of one-sided observation needs to stop because it does not help foster a school climate that focuses on learning as much as it sets up a school climate focused on compliance.

As noted in Figure 4.1, leaders coconstruct a goal with each staff member before an observation. This process will allow the leader to provide better feedback because we know that feedback is best when it is attached to a goal.

I heard from many leaders and teachers that the process made their observations more impactful. Even something as simple as coconstructing or asking a teacher to define a goal prior to the actual observation made the process more authentic for teachers and leaders. However, during some productive conversations some teachers stated it may not fit

Figure 4.1   Cycle of Collaborative Teacher Observation

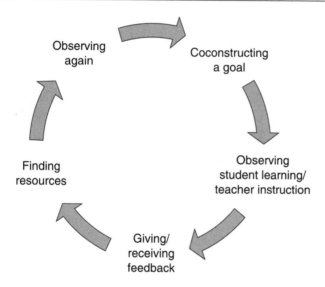

into their annual professional performance review (APPR), which is their formal teacher evaluation process. The APPR process looks different depending on state or country.

First and foremost, if teachers and leaders are going to work together, they do have to establish protocols of protection because we know that not all leaders are created equally. Protocols of protection, otherwise known as contracts, help teachers who may find themselves with a principal who rules with an iron fist. However, the teacher union side should also be flexible. Both sides have been somewhat responsible for observations that have provided little feedback. The teacher evaluation process should involve language that will give leaders and teachers the flexibility they need to make the observation more of a cycle (i.e., one formal observation and one follow-up walkthrough).

In order for this cycle to work, leaders and teachers should decide on what part fits into the formal process developed by their state education department or ministry of education, and what part will have flexibility to allow for improvement. For example, perhaps the formal aspect to the APPR process is when the teacher and leader coconstruct a goal, the leader does a formal evidence-based observation, and then provides feedback. Research has shown that the section in which the principal observes the teacher can be as short as 20 minutes and still be effective (Gargani & Strong, 2014).

The part that may remain outside the formal written process is when the leader continues to help the teacher by providing resources that will better assist the teacher in the strategies he or she uses to build student engagement, or when the leader goes back into the classroom to see the learned strategy in use and provides more feedback that may be more along the line of coaching or appreciative feedback (Stone & Heen, 2015).

In my lifetime, I would enjoy seeing this model replicated by schools so that teachers and leaders can engage in a cycle of improvement together. The process described earlier and the conversations that take place during it are effective ways to increase the likelihood of a supportive and inclusive school climate. Although I have used these tips in previous work, I think they are important to highlight again when thinking about the cycle of collaborative observation.

Tips for Creating Better Collaborative Observations

- Have the meeting in the teacher's classroom instead of your office.
- Encourage teachers to create their goal. *Don't do it for them.*
- Help teachers find *one* article, blog, or link to a video.
- Keep a file listing each teacher's goal.
- Leaders should share their goal. Get teacher input on what the goal should be.

Additional to the cycle and these tips, there are questions that leaders and teachers can use in preobservation meetings as well as postobservation meetings.

Collaborative Preconference Questions

- What are you hoping the students will learn?
- How will students know the learning intention of the lesson?
- How will students know they're successful after the lesson is finished?
- If you could paint a picture of student engagement, what would it look like?
- How do you know when the students are authentically engaged more than compliantly engaged?
- What are some questions you hope students will ask?
- What evidence will you collect to understand your impact?
- Are you having any challenges you need my help with?

Collaborative Postconference Questions

- On a scale of 1 to 10, how close did the lesson come to reaching your goal (Knight, 2007)?
- What would have to change to make it closer to a 10 (Knight, 2007)?
- What evidence did you collect to show student growth?
- Besides the strategy you used, is there another one you have been hoping to try?
- Is there a different teaching strategy you would use to achieve a higher impact on student learning?
- When I go in to observe the next lesson, how will I be able to see how the learning has been enhanced?

It is my hope that the cycle and all of the parts of it will help increase better conversations between leaders and teachers. If we can start with improving our collaborative observations, imagine what we can do with professional development, teacher leadership, and our small communities of learning that include collaborative inquiry. All of these are important elements to how collaborative leaders work with teachers and are necessary elements of school climate.

Professional Learning and Development (PLD)

Unfortunately, the last few years of increased mandates and accountability have set up a dynamic in which the self-efficacy of teachers has been lowered. It seems as though, in countries such as the United States, Australia, and the United Kindgom, teachers lack the autonomy they once had, and it has been replaced with accountability instead. In other countries such as Finland, where they have always fared well on the Programme for International Student Assessment (PISA), teachers are treated like professionals and have a great deal of autonomy, which is linked to the academic and social-emotional growth of their students.

Don't get me wrong, I do not want to go back to the days when teachers closed their classroom doors behind them and were left to their own devices. However, I don't want to see countries continue to increase accountability, which has not worked so well when it comes to achievement (Fullan & Hargreaves, 2016). This all results in a loss of self-efficacy (Lopez & Sidhu, 2013; Quaglia & Lande, 2017).

Self-efficacy is the "confidence or strength of belief that we have in ourselves that we can make our learning happen" (Hattie, 2012a) and "refers to beliefs in one's capabilities to organize and execute the courses of action required to produce given attainments" (Bandura, 1997, p. 3). Teacher efficacy, which I will be focusing on in most of this chapter, refers to the "extent to which teachers believe that they have the capacity to affect student performance" (Ashton, Webb, & Doda, 1982, p. 9). In a powerful doctoral dissertation titled *Meta-Analysis of the Relationship Between Collective Teacher Efficacy and Student Achievement* (2011), Eells cited Ashton and Webb (1986) when writing,

Teachers with low teaching efficacy don't feel that teachers, in general, can make much of a difference in the lives of students, while teachers with low personal teaching efficacy don't feel that they, personally, affect the lives of the students. (p. 37)

All of this information we are continuing to learn about self-efficacy, teacher efficacy, and collective teacher efficacy, which is the "perceptions of teachers in a school that the efforts of the faculty as a whole will have a positive impact on students" (Goddard, Hoy, & Woolfolk Hoy, 2000, p. 479) is important because, done correctly, it can have an enormous impact on school climate.

Teacher Efficacy Scale (Short Form)*

Hoy and Woolfolk (1993) offer a more in-depth efficacy scale for teachers to fill out. With their permission, here are some of the questions from their scale, along with the website to visit for further information if leaders and teachers want to explore teacher efficacy further.

Instructions: Please indicate your personal opinion about each statement by circling the appropriate response to the right of each statement.

Key: 1 = Strongly agree, 2 = Moderately agree, 3 = Agree slightly more than disagree, 4 = Disagree slightly more than agree, 5 = Moderately disagree, 6 = Strongly disagree

The amount a student can learn is primarily related to family background.	1	2	3	4	5	6
If students aren't disciplined at home, they aren't likely to accept any discipline.	1	2	3	4	5	6

(Continued)

(Continued)

When I really try, I can get through to most difficult students.	1	2	3	4	5	6
A teacher is very limited in what he or she can achieve because a student's home environment is a large influence on his or her achievement.	1	2	3	4	5	6
If parents would do more for their children, I could do more.	1	2	3	4	5	6

Source: Hoy, W. K., & Woolfolk, A. E. (1993). Teachers' sense of efficacy and the organizational health of schools. The Elementary School Journal 93, 356–372.

*For more information on this scale, visit http://u.osu.edu/hoy.17/research/instruments and http://www.waynekhoy.com/collective_efficacy.html

We should no longer be taking away the decision-making power of teachers because we begin to enable them and not empower them, which also has a negative impact on teacher voice (Quaglia & Lande, 2017). In fact, Lopez and Sidhu (2013) found that out of any occupation, teachers were less likely to believe their voice mattered in decision-making in school. In their study involving more than 12,000 teachers, Quaglia and Lande (2015) found "that only 59% of teachers are comfortable expressing their honest opinions and concerns" (p. 10). This statistic matters greatly because Quaglia and Lande (2015) also found that "teachers who are comfortable expressing honest opinions and concerns are four times more likely to be excited about their future careers in education," and "when teachers have a voice in decision making, they are four times more likely to believe they can make a difference. They are also three times more likely to encourage students to be leaders and to make decisions" (p. 10).

Stop. Collaborate and Listen!

According to Quaglia and Lande (2015), there are action steps leaders can take to foster teacher voice. A few of those action steps are as follows:

Establish a teacher mentoring program: Veteran teachers are assigned to support new teachers in order to "help build a culture of mutual trust" (p. 19).

Post the hopes and dreams of staff members: In the faculty room, post the hopes and dreams about schooling where colleagues can listen and learn from one another.

Communication skills: Quaglia and Lande support the idea of spending 10 minutes of each staff meeting focusing on communication skills among colleagues.

Create a professional learning board: "Designate a bulletin board in a public area of the school where teachers can share something they learned from a colleague" (p. 19).

One of the most common ways to increase the volume on teacher voice is through professional learning and development. Fullan and Hargreaves write, "Professional learning is often like student learning—something that is deliberately structured and increasingly accepted because it can (to some) more obviously be linked to measurable outcomes" (2016, p. 3).

Campbell and colleagues (2016, p. 8) found, "Generally, professional learning content needs to develop teachers' efficacy, knowledge, and practices in order to support students' efficacy, engagement, learning, and equity of outcomes."

Fullan and Hargreaves (2016) go on to define *professional development* as the "many aspects of learning but may also involve developing mindfulness, team building and team development, intellectual stimulation for its own sake, reading good literature that prompts reflection on the human condition" (p. 4).

Therefore, professional learning and development combine both of those constructs to make for more powerful learning. Based on the research by Quaglia and Lande (2017), we can see why teachers may feel as though professional development is done to them rather than with them. Instead of engaging in professional development that is anything but engaging, we need to engage in PLD that can be flexible and powerful. However, it means leaders have to be open to different types of learning—for example, using badges for teachers to increase their self-efficacy. The vignette by Ned Dale on badges encompasses research from Fullan and Hargreaves (2016) as well as Campbell and her team (2016).

Practitioner's Voice

Using Badges to Build Teacher Self-Efficacy

Ned Dale, Middle School Principal
Cosgrove Middle School
Spencerport, New York

When I first learned that our superintendent accepted the recommendation to move to a 1:1 computing environment within a two-year time span, I immediately thought about the needs of our faculty. I have led our 21st Century Team of teachers for the past five years through a series of obstacles and transitions with technology. We went from banning cell phones to an open BYOD program and now to a 1:1 program. My main goals were always to create a support system for our staff through in-house professional development, as well seek out best practices and new applications that come in faster than I can keep up with.

In the 2015–2016 school year, we piloted and selected a learning management system (LMS) as we prepared for the 1:1 initiative. How would I support teachers with this huge endeavor and significant change? The district office professional development department created course offerings that allowed people to move through various levels to learn "schoology." I enrolled in the first course and picked up much of the logistics of this intuitive program. During the second course, I learned and was intrigued about the use and wealth of resources and ways to engage students, specifically about badges.

Badges are thumbnail images representing the personal quality, task, or behavior that you can assign to a teacher's (or student's) account. For example, an individual can earn a leadership, participation, positive attitude, or lifelong learner badge. I had read a recent tweet and blog about the success of gamification within the new generation of students that would rapidly enter our middle school. I planned to roll out and model the use of our learning management system to the entire staff in September. In addition to running most faculty meetings through this program, I began to assign badges once the staff completed various tasks. After the first meeting, each staff member successfully logged on and participated in an online discussion and assessment, as well uploaded a paperless reflection that outlined goals for the year. I awarded badges for these tasks, with a few people noticing.

As we continued through the year, I began awarding leadership badges when I noted countless faculty members taking on leadership opportunities. A few more began noticing the badges. As the 21st Century Team began preparing for a faculty workshop that would allow the staff to select one of eight breakout sessions, we had a discussion about how to structure them and then build time for the staff to implement their learning. The group wanted to make sure that people were able to be successful with their learning. Immediately, I went and created another badge with the plan that the administrative team would award a badge based on the integration of their learning that would be noted as evidence within our walkthrough observations. We began to explicitly point out the use of the badges within our learning management system and how they could be earned. One staff member said, "We are just like kids—we like to earn the badges for what we do well." In addition, we challenged the staff with coming up how they could use them within their own classes.

We have a lot more to learn about using badges to improve the self-efficacy of our faculty, but I am going to test the waters to see if we can encourage more people to integrate their learning from professional development that is building based.

Badges are not about a one and done. In Ned's school, badges are used to build collective efficacy among staff, and teachers get to share their strengths and help those that might find the same thing to be a weakness. If one teacher is strong at using a Smart board in the classroom and she or he flawlessly uses it daily with students, and another teacher is still putting worksheets on his or her Smart board, they can get together to learn from each other. Badges can be distributed based on whether someone has a basic, proficient, or advanced understanding.

Ned's story about badges is similar to the way that Tim Cooper would run a professional development session because it is based in trust. It is quite possible that Trudy Cowen would do the same thing, but highly likely that she would make teachers fill out a form and prove their learning. Just remember, as it was when teachers had to hand in lesson plans that were not really looked at, we might assume that Trudy will not read the forms. It is important, however, that regardless of how you approach a professional development structure such as badges, that feedback is provided on whatever teachers submit.

Besides the use of badges, which is clearly a great way to engage in professional learning and development at the same time the collaborative leader increases the volume on teacher voice, there are other ways leaders are finding to inspire teachers to collaborate. One of the other ways to foster self-efficacy and engage in building collective teacher efficacy is through the use of teacher leaders.

Teacher Leaders and School Climate

Do we need teacher leaders? Where do we find them? Do we groom them, or do they come to us already eager to be put in that position? Are they the teachers who are shy with their colleagues but excel in the classroom with their students? Or are they the teachers who give leaders feedback even at times when the leaders aren't open to hearing it? The truth is, and you probably know this already, our teacher leaders are all of these things.

Teacher leaders, self-efficacy, and collective teacher efficacy are all interrelated (see Figure 4.2).

Figure 4.2   Circle of Teacher Leaders, Self-Efficacy, and Collective Teacher Efficacy

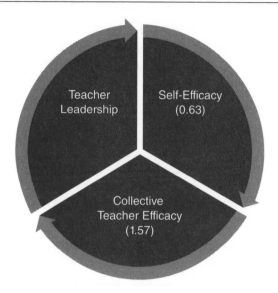

All teachers need self-efficacy so they can work together to build collective teacher efficacy, and we often need teacher leaders to help support the initial learning and keep the momentum going. Teacher leaders can help their colleagues understand their current reality and establish a goal to help them improve on that current reality (Knight, 2007). The aspect in which teacher leaders have a benefit that school leaders often do not is that teacher leaders aren't responsible for evaluating staff. Therefore, more teachers may be much more open and honest with the teacher leader because their evaluations aren't at risk.

This concept of teacher leadership seems to be growing in popularity. However, teacher leadership is not new because teachers have always been considered as leaders in their own classrooms (Lai & Chueng, 2015). Lai and Cheung found that there are four different types of teacher leadership to consider.

Teacher Leadership

1. **Can be individually or collectively based:** The position takes place because colleagues go to the teacher for support naturally, or a principal sees the leadership qualities within the teacher and the role is more formal.

2. **Is transformational in nature:** The teacher leader is in the position to help change the culture of the school and therefore can help to create a better school climate for students and colleagues.

3. **Functions in communities of practice:** Cheung says, "When teachers lead, they engage colleagues and other members of a school community in examining individual and collective teaching practices and the school's programs and policies" (p. 675).

4. **Supports school development at different levels:** The overarching goal of any teacher leader is to focus on student learning. (p. 675)

Lai and Cheung's (2015) four roles of teacher leaders can be beneficial when we consider professional learning and development, especially those concepts furthered by Fullan and Hargreaves (2016) and Campbell and colleagues (2016). Additionally, this can help shift the conversation from focusing on teaching and the adults in the room to focusing on students and the learning that takes place within the room and outside the school walls.

Why is this an important aspect to collaborative leadership and school climate? I began this book by writing that it is well-documented that leadership has an important impact on school improvement (Hallinger & Heck, 1996; Leithwood et al., 2004). That leadership goes beyond collaborative leaders to the teachers within the building. A high-quality school climate where teachers are working together with the leader is the ultimate goal for any collaborative leader. Imagine the student learning we can inspire if the adults are all working together!

Too often, teacher leaders are seen as assistant principals, which makes the position complicated because for it to be successful the administrator and teacher leader need to have a positive relationship (Angelle & DeHart, 2011). However, in many buildings teacher leaders, as well as instructional coaches, are seen as compliance officers, used to carry out the mission of the leader and make sure that teachers are pacing with one another.

Additionally, the compliance officer mentality carries through when professional learning and development is compliance based and does not focus on the collaborative sharing of teachers around coconstructed goals to help improve the climate of learning in classrooms and the school. In the following vignette, Principal Carolyn Rafferty explains how she looks past compliance and focuses on building collective efficacy.

Practitioner's Voice

Be Ready for the Long Haul

Carolyn Rafferty, Principal
Stall Brook Elementary School
Bellingham, Massachusetts

Building teacher efficacy, and eventually collective efficacy, takes time and patience. In my role as principal at the Stall Brook Elementary School in Bellingham, Massachusetts, I have had the privilege of watching 11 professionals transition from a group to a working team and ultimately into a high-functioning instructional leadership team.

The development of our instructional leadership team (ILT) has proven to be an effective vehicle for fostering teacher and collective efficacy. Our team consists of 11 members of the schoolwide staff, including classroom teachers, special education teachers, and our literacy and math specialists. I began the process of building the team with an open invitation to

(Continued)

(Continued)

the staff as a whole. When there proved to be limited interest, I personally sought out teachers that I had observed to be highly motivated to try new ideas in their classrooms, teachers that were highly reflective in their practice, and teachers that were openly collaborating with others to improve their own repertoire of instructional practices. The personal invitation and the acknowledgement of the work that *they* were already doing made the difference.

The first year of our work together as an ILT was spent establishing norms for our group. We learned how to put ideas forward and to be comfortable pulling them back when needed. We learned to probe for specificity and assume positive intentions. These norms soon became embedded into our meeting protocols. We also spent time focusing on understanding each other's personal preferences for approaching work as strengths, to understand others rather than judge them, and to be more self-aware using a protocol called Compass Points, adapted from National School Reform Faculty (www.nsrfharmony.org). This work made it possible for us to engage in effective communication and constructive conflict.

The second year of our work together focused on analyzing school-wide data to determine our student learning needs. We also conducted a self-survey using the Conditions of School Effectiveness (https://www2.ed.gov/about/inits/ed/implementation-support-unit/tech-assist/ma-essential.pdf). Massachusetts' Essential Conditions for School Effectiveness articulate the key elements that the state believes every school needs to have in place for all students to succeed.

We met for a full day each month, building our capacity as a team and slowly bringing about changes in instructional practices through the use of Learning Walkthroughs, professional readings, schedule changes, and increased time for collaboration at the individual grade levels. Each month, we looked at student learning data and listened to the needs voiced by the staff in the building. Along the way, we adopted what we called "nonnegotiable practices" that we expected to see in every classroom at every grade level, based on the research we had engaged in and a site visit we made to a high-performing school in another part of the state.

Learning Walkthroughs were one way of progress monitoring the work that we were doing. During these walks and the debriefing sessions that followed, we began to see more and more evidence of the instructional practices we agreed upon being implemented at the classroom level. Staff outside of the ILT grew increasingly curious about the work that was being done, and the ILT became more and more influential at their grade level meetings, sharing the work they were engaged in, which inevitably led to increased commitment to the initiatives.

Reflecting on the process, I attribute the success of the instructional leadership team to the level of voice it gave the staff. It provided a vehicle for teachers to be heard and for the collective group to move forward on initiatives that came from the work they were doing. At a recent workshop I attended with the team, the presenter asked the group why they were on ILTs. I asked my staff why they were *still* on the team. The answer—"Because we still have work to do!"—made it clear to me they see themselves as having the ability to make positive things happen.

The vignette from Carolyn illustrates how approaching situations from a collaborative mindset will help create a school climate that focuses on learning rather than compliance.

Whether it's running professional learning and development or using teacher leaders as curriculum leaders across grade levels and departments or using them to engage in collaborative inquiry, it is really important for leaders to understand why teacher leadership is important and for them to decide what they want out of teacher leaders. And lastly and equally important, *their leaders* need to support them as they go through the teacher leadership process.

Building Collective Efficacy Through Collaborative Inquiry

In looking at additional ways to build the collective efficacy of staff and to foster a school climate that focuses on learning, collaborative leaders can engage in one of the most effective ways of fostering the strengths of staff members—the process of collaborative inquiry. But what does collaborative inquiry look like?

Two examples follow. The first is from Sarah Martin, the school leader at Stonefields School in Auckland, New Zealand. Sarah and the staff at Stonefields are the epitome of what it looks like to build collective efficacy, and they do it through a collaborative inquiry–type approach. I have visited Stonefields, and it's an amazing learning environment for students.

Practitioner's Voice

Building Synergy and Stonefields

Sarah Martin, Principal
Stonefields School
Auckland, New Zealand

Stonefields School opened its doors to a vibrant community of learners at the beginning of 2011. It currently has a roll of 600 learners, which continues to grow by approximately 100 new learners each year. One of the most significant decisions made early on was that teachers wouldn't be assigned their own class; rather, three teachers would work collaboratively to design and cause learning, and they would use one another's strengths to serve their 75 to 80 learners.

Our most significant impact is directly correlated to our highest-functioning teams because they have accelerated impact on learner outcomes. We have come to call these teams *synergetic* because they operate with conviction; have a clear, shared purpose; and relentlessly drive toward ensuring their learners' progress and achievements. There is no deficit thinking—in fact, quite the contrary: Curiosity and evaluation result in constant evolving practice to better serve the learners that might not be making optimal progress.

Collective efficacy is at the heart of a synergetic team. It is quite intentional that there is no leadership within a learning hub; different individuals play to their strengths to provide informal leadership when desired. Such leadership comes and goes as a new shared purpose, problem, or crisis comes to bear.

Most teams do not become synergetic overnight. We have continued to inquire why some teams function so effectively and some never reach the same level of effectiveness. We have been looking into what elements underpin high-functioning teams and whether these can also be developed in teams that are less effective. This has continued to be an important question, as we now know the potential impact that collective efficacy has on learner outcomes.

Intentional professional learning and practices have been discovered as Stonefields has continued to evolve in a strategically organic way. Many frameworks and tools have been created to use with teams to reflect on their level of function individually and as a collective group. A model with accompanying continuums has been developed to help teams evaluate where they are, reflect on the evidence that suggests why they're there, and think about where they would like to be and what will help them get there.

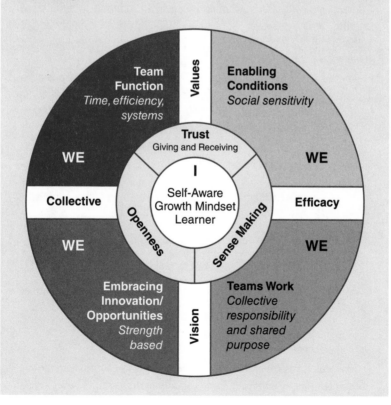

The second example of collaborative inquiry comes from a blog I coauthored with Jenni Donohoo, who is the author of *Collective Efficacy: How Educators' Beliefs Impact Student Learning* (2016). Donohoo, in my opinion, is one of the world's foremost experts on collaborative inquiry.

Why Collaborative Inquiry? Professional Learning That Makes a Difference

Peter DeWitt and Jenni Donohoo (2016)

November 20, 2016
Finding Common Ground Blog—blogs.edweek.org

The term *job-embedded* is commonplace when referring to professional learning today; however, sometimes "job-embedded" simply entails a change in location—a move from ballrooms into school libraries or gymnasiums.

At other times, the term is used to mask top-down, directive approaches under the guise of increased teacher choice and autonomy. In order for professional learning to make a difference, we need to define *job-embedded* and consider aspects that make professional learning impactful.

This article contains five key ideas for educators to consider. Professional learning is powerful when

1. *Learning* is defined as a change in thinking and behaviour (Katz & Dack, 2013).

2. The power of the collective is drawn upon.

3. Teachers' influence and power to make decisions are increased.

4. Results are interpreted and cause/effect relationships are identified.

5. A staff's perception of their ability to affect change is positively influenced.

The premise is that when educators engage in continuous learning, student learning is improved. However, not all professional development leads to *learning* as defined by Katz and Dack as a "permanent change in thinking and behaviour" (2013, p. vii).

Realizing improved outcomes for *all* students requires that educators examine and question long-standing fundamental beliefs and make permanent changes to their practice by trying, assessing, and reflecting upon the effectiveness of different teaching strategies and approaches. Therefore, it is important to structure and provide professional development that sets the bar, based on Katz and Dack's definition of *learning*. Professional learning makes a difference when it results in permanent changes in thinking and behaviour.

A second consideration in designing professional learning involves drawing upon the power of the collective—what Hargreaves and Fullan (2012) refer to as "social capital." The authors argued that in order to accelerate learning it is important to concentrate on the group and noted that "social capital strategies are one of the cornerstones for transforming the profession" (p. 91).

Professional learning structures and processes that require educators to collaborate in order to identify and solve problems of practice are what is needed. "High-yield strategies become more precise and more embedded when they are developed and deployed in teams that are constantly refining and interpreting them" (Hargreaves & Fullan, 2012, p. 96). In my experience, educators' most valuable professional learning is a result of in-depth collaboration.

Effective professional learning also increases teachers' influence and their power to make decisions on important issues related to school improvement and professional learning. Leadership opportunities extend beyond merely serving on a committee or acting as a department or division chair. Structures for teachers to become authentic leaders and decision-makers need to be in place. Through their leadership, collaborative work, and meaningful involvement in school improvement, teachers become catalysts for change.

When educators' everyday work and student learning are examined as rich sources of evidence, professional learning is more constructive and truly "embedded in daily practice" (a phrase I prefer over "job-embedded"). Educators collaboratively analyze student evidence for the purpose of evaluating their impact, reflecting on their collective work,

(Continued)

(Continued)

and determining optimal next steps. Interpreting results by examining student learning data helps to strengthen connections between the learning task, content, instruction, and student outcomes.

When conversations shift from generalized talk about students' progress and polite sharing of teaching strategies to more in-depth conversations about the connections between the two, professional learning becomes more impactful. This shift can only occur in light of student learning data.

Finally, professional learning becomes more powerful when it is intentionally designed to influence a staff's perception of their ability to positively influence student outcomes. With an effect size of 1.57, Hattie (2016) recently ranked collective teacher efficacy (CTE) as the *number-one* factor influencing student achievement. Collective teacher efficacy refers to the "collective self-perception that teachers in a given school make an educational difference to their students over and above the educational impact of their homes and communities" (Tschannen-Moran & Barr, 2004, p. 190).

Efficacy beliefs are very powerful, as they "directly affect the diligence and resolve with which groups choose to pursue their goals" (Goddard, Hoy, & Woolfolk Hoy, 2004, p.8). When teachers believe that together they are capable of helping students master complex content, fostering students' creativity, and getting students to believe they can do well in school, it happens. If educators' realities are filtered through the belief that there is very little they can do to influence student achievement, then it is very likely these beliefs will be manifested in their practice.

Professional learning makes a difference when it purposefully and explicitly taps into the sources of collective efficacy (mastery experiences, vicarious experiences, social persuasion, and affective states). Furthermore, when professional learning is designed to assist teachers in making the link between *their* collective actions and increases in student achievement, it helps in fostering collective efficacy (Donohoo, 2016).

Collaborative inquiry is a professional learning design that makes a difference by delivering on the five aspects that make professional learning impactful, outlined earlier. Katz and Dack (2013) argued that conceptual change is necessary for fundamental school improvement and noted that collaborative inquiry is an "enabler of the kind of professional learning that is about permanent change in thinking or behaviour" (p. 7).

Changes in beliefs occur as teachers reconcile discrepancies between initial thinking and new ideas that emerge through the examination of evidence and reflection (Donohoo & Velasco, 2016). Transfer is more likely to occur when teachers build knowledge together. Interdependence of action and connections with other educators ultimately influence changes in practice.

Collaborative inquiry situates educators' everyday work as the central focus for their learning. Educators' encounters rest on a shared responsibility for improving student outcomes, and interdependence results from the need to draw upon each other's experience and expertise in order to develop more common understandings of student learning needs and instructional practices. In addition, the collaborative inquiry process has been found particularly effective in increasing efficacy (Bruce & Flynn, 2013; Voelkel Jr., 2011).

Given limited time and resources, it makes sense to concentrate professional learning efforts on designs that make a difference. Collaborative inquiry is one such design that not only makes a difference in regard to student outcomes but also results in greater buy-in from educators.

The cycle of collaborative observation, professional learning and development, and collaborative inquiry are all important aspects of school climate because they often are a requirement of all staff. If teachers are inspired through the collaborative observation process, professional learning and development, and collaborative inquiry, they could have a powerful impact on students.

Classroom Climate

The classroom climate is probably not something many leaders think about because they are focused on the overall school climate. However, each classroom climate is a piece of the much-larger puzzle, and research shows the classroom environment has a 0.53 effect size. When teachers and students are learning together using learning intentions and success criteria, there will be more positive gains in growth and achievement.

Teachers with a higher level of self-efficacy will most likely have students who are much more engaged in learning because self-efficacy is about understanding the ability we have to help inspire others. Teachers with less self-efficacy may be more likely to have classroom management issues, students who are frequent flyers to the principal's office, and students who do not grow as much as they could.

When I was a teacher, I believed that everyone must teach like I did. It's not that I believed I was a talented teacher, but I did care about the climate of the classroom. I wanted students to have a place they could come to learn but also escape from home lives that were not magical. I played music for transitions between centers and painted the back wall to emulate a magic tree house. I used fine art from Monet, Manet, John Singer Sargent, and Camille Corot to inspire students to write, and I cotaught with special education teachers whom I wanted to feel at home because I noticed their previous experiences with other teachers did not help build collective efficacy. The special education teachers I cotaught with in previous experiences were not allowed much of a voice in the classrooms and spent most of their time pulling their classified students out or standing behind those students, pointing at what to do next on the worksheet.

When I became a principal, I realized not all classrooms were the same. Some had soft lighting to minimize the harmful nature of fluorescent lighting and exercise balls for students to sit, while other classrooms were places where students had to sit quietly, raise their hands when they needed something, and were sometimes worried to speak up. Don't get me wrong— I loved working with all of the teachers, but some didn't allow as much voice as others.

Rowe, Sangwon, Baker, Kamphaus, and Horne (2010) define *classroom climate* as "the classroom social atmosphere (B. Johnson & McClure, 2004) or the social–psychological environment for learning (Fraser, 1994)" (p. 860). Collaborative leaders need to keep in mind that the experience for each student is different when it comes to classroom climate. In a study of elementary students, Rowe and her colleagues found that "two students in the same class may have very different relationships with their teacher. As a result, their personal experience of teacher support in the class could be different" (2010, p. 860).

There are so many hot-button issues that we need to be able to talk through that revolve around race, gender, and sexual orientation, but in many classrooms, those conversations will never take place. The conversations won't take place for several reasons, including the fact that teachers will not discuss what makes them uncomfortable. Those conversations also won't take place because sometimes teachers who would like to explore them with students do not feel as though they have administrative support, and other times, they won't take place because teachers and leaders are concerned about parental pushback.

If schools are to be places where all students feel included, then we as educators need to have conversations, read books, engage in debates, and hang up posters and artwork that depict the very students who attend our schools and depict the very population that lives within our country. When teachers engage in this positive behavior that includes all students, they will see increased engagement among their students. In elementary, middle, and high school studies, researchers found that students are more engaged when they believe their teachers like them (Hattie, 2009; Quaglia & Lande, 2015; Shernoff, Ruzek, & Sinha, 2016).

Collaborative leaders can look to many of the influences that will help them focus on a more inclusive and engaging classroom climate. For example, teacher–student relationships have an effect size of 0.72, which is well over the hinge point of 0.40 (equal to a year's worth of growth for a year's input). However, there are many other influences that leaders can focus on when they collaborate with teachers during the cycle of collaborative teacher observation, professional learning and development, and collaborative inquiry. Figure 4.3 illustrates some of Hattie's (2012a) high-impact strategies that can be used when considering classroom climate.

Figure 4.3   Classroom Climate

Teacher credibility	0.90
Providing formative evaluation	0.90
Classroom discussion	0.82
Teacher–student relationships	0.72
Classroom behavior	0.68
Not labeling students	0.61
Student-centered teaching	0.54
Motivation	0.48
Cooperative learning	0.42
Reducing anxiety	0.40

Source: Hattie (2012a).

In the End

Collaborative leaders need to keep exploring some of the big areas addressed in this chapter because as much as we may be moving forward to increasing teacher and student voice, we still have a long way to go because of the damage that has been created from too many mandates and accountability measures. We need to stop looking at leadership as if those who are in it went to the "dark side," which means those in leadership positions have to work harder to lower their status as leaders and raise the status for those around them. Raising the status of those around us will help increase their level of self-efficacy and build collective teacher efficacy.

How do we do that? We engage in the cycle of collaborative observation in which we work with teachers toward a goal that matters. We understand the current reality of our teachers and help provide feedback that will help them improve, no matter how good they are, so that they walk away finally feeling as if the observation process is done with them and not to them. We fully engage in walkthroughs when we have more than simple "look-fors" but actually step in, talk with students, and see if they are heavily engaged in what it looks like they're engaged in.

Being more collaborative means that we engage in the professional learning and development model that Fullan and Hargreaves (2016) have written about and researched, and we explore more flexible ways of doing it like that of Ned Dale from Spencerport, New York. If we want teachers to be lifelong learners, then our PLD should be inspiring and not stifling. And one of the ways to make learning more powerful is through Donohoo's (2016) collaborative inquiry approach to learning. In my opinion, Donohoo's model helps highlight the fact that teaching is filled with professionals who are engaged in research and high-impact strategies that focus on student learning.

Lastly, we have to work on each classroom climate with the understanding that each child reacts differently to the same climate (B. Johnson & McClure, 2004). Classroom climates are an integral part of the overall school climate that we should be focusing on every day. We should be talking at faculty meetings and in our formal conversations about whether students feel supported in the classroom. We should be asking teachers about the ways they build relationships with students, which we know has a 0.72 effect size in Hattie's work.

Leadership is difficult because we constantly feel like plate spinners—and as soon as we have all plates spinning, we are constantly watching for the first one to fall off the stick because leadership is about being the spinner and the stick all at the same time.

One of the last parts to creating the school community that can often be the most complicated is how we engage with families. Collaborative leadership is not just about how we work with those stakeholders within the school walls but also how we engage those outside the school walls as well because learning and issues around learning (i.e., academic, social-emotional) do not stop when the bell rings.

ACTION STEPS

- Encourage teachers to create a goal, or coconstruct one with them, before your next formal, evidence-based observation cycle.
- Make sure you provide one piece of feedback no matter how great the lesson goes. If the teacher was highly engaging, try to find one extension activity to help them be even more engaging.
- Understand the self-efficacy (0.63) of individual teachers and use PLD, faculty meetings, and observations as a way to build collective teacher efficacy (1.57).
- Offer flexibility when it comes to professional learning and development. Are badges something you can use?
- Research Ontario, Canada-based Donohoo's work on collaborative inquiry for teachers.
- Read Carol Campbell's full report on professional learning and development in Canada. We may live in different countries, but we can learn a lot from one another.
- Discuss school climate and classroom climate with teachers in faculty meetings, PLCs, or one-to-one conversations.

DISCUSSION QUESTIONS

- How is your present observation cycle different from the cycle of collaborative observation? How are they the same?
- Think of a recent conversation with a teacher that went badly. What could you have done differently?
- Think of an upcoming conversation. How will you listen and respond more openly?
- In what ways do you help teachers turn up the volume on their voice in school?
- What is professional learning and development?
- What is collaborative inquiry? Have you used it?
- How important is classroom climate to the overall climate of your school?

TRUDY AND TIM

- Out of all of the examples provided in this chapter, if you were Trudy, which one would you work on first in order to become more collaborative?
- How might Tim approach collaborative inquiry with his teachers?

Collective Teacher Efficacy Scale

Below is a collective teacher efficacy scale by Megan Tschannen-Moran, College of William and Mary. The scoring directions are included. In order to find the full collective teacher efficacy scale, please visit http://wmpeople.wm.edu/site/page/mxtsch/researchtools.

	None at All		Very Little		Some Degree		Quite a Bit		A Great Deal
1. How much can teachers in your school do to produce meaningful student learning?	1	2	3	4	5	6	7	8	9
2. How much can your school do to get students to believe they can do well in schoolwork?	1	2	3	4	5	6	7	8	9
3. To what extent can teachers in your school make expectations clear about appropriate student behavior?	1	2	3	4	5	6	7	8	9
4. To what extent can school personnel in your school establish rules and procedures that facilitate learning?	1	2	3	4	5	6	7	8	9
5. How much can teachers in your school do to help students master complex content?	1	2	3	4	5	6	7	8	9
6. How much can teachers in your school do to promote deep understanding of academic concepts?	1	2	3	4	5	6	7	8	9

	None at All	**Very Little**	**Some Degree**	**Quite a Bit**	**A Great Deal**
7. How well can teachers in your school respond to defiant students?	1 2	3 4	5 6	7 8	9
8. How much can school personnel in your school do to control disruptive behavior?	1 2	3 4	5 6	7 8	9
9. How much can teachers in your school do to help students think critically?	1 2	3 4	5 6	7 8	9
10. How well can adults in your school get students to follow school rules?	1 2	3 4	5 6	7 8	9
11. How much can your school do to foster student creativity?	1 2	3 4	5 6	7 8	9
12. How much can your school do to help students feel safe while they are at school?	1 2	3 4	5 6	7 8	9

Developer: Megan Tschannen-Moran, College of William and Mary. Tschannen-Moran, M., & Barr, M. (2004). Fostering Student Learning: The Relationship of Collective Teacher Efficacy and Student Achievement. *Leadership and Policy in Schools, 3*(3), 189–209.

Directions for Scoring the Collective Teacher Efficacy Scale

Construct Validity

Construct validity of the Collective Teacher Efficacy Scale was established through factor analysis. Two strong factors emerge that were moderately correlated. When a second-order factor analysis was conducted, the two factors formed a single factor.

(Continued)

(Continued)

Subscale Scores

An overall collective teacher efficacy score can be computed by taking a mean of all 12 items. To determine the *Collective Efficacy in Instructional Strategies* and the *Collective Efficacy in Student Discipline* subscale scores, compute a mean score of the items that relate to each factor.

Instructional Strategies

1. How much can teachers in your school do to produce meaningful student learning?

2. How much can your school do to get students to believe they can do well in schoolwork?

3. How much can teachers in your school do to help students master complex content?

4. How much can teachers in your school do to promote deep understanding of academic concepts?

5. How much can teachers in your school do to help students think critically?

6. How much can your school do to foster student creativity?

Student Discipline

7. To what extent can teachers in your school make expectations clear about appropriate student behavior?

8. To what extent can school personnel in your school establish rules and procedures that facilitate learning?

9. How well can teachers in your school respond to defiant students?

10. How much can school personnel in your school do to control disruptive behavior?

11. How well can adults in your school get students to follow school rules?

12. How much can your school do to help students feel safe while they are at school?

5

Building Collective Efficacy With Families

Most people do not listen with the intent to understand; they listen with the intent to reply.

—Stephen Covey

What do we want out of our relationships with families? What are our expectations for them? Some people don't like the word *expectations*, but many teachers and leaders have expectations of families. Sometimes, those expectations are set so high that parents can't possibly live up to them, and other times, they're set so low they are disrespectful to parents and demeaning to children. As much as we have many families who are there to support their children—and a few that seem to want to put their children in bubble wrap so nothing bad happens to them—we also have families that never want to be involved. It's easy for us to judge the families who are too involved and those who are not involved enough. One of my former leaders told me that families are sending in the best kids they have and are doing the best job they know how to do.

Remember, families who seem as though they don't care may have come from families who didn't care either. We can help them break the cycle.

Truth be told, I grew up in a family that didn't always feel connected to the teachers and principals in our school community. We came from the west end of town, which wasn't the most affluent, and that contributed to that disconnect we felt from school. However, we also suffered from a lack of self-efficacy as well. There were many reasons for this, but one of the biggest and most profound was that my dad passed away when I was 11. When that happens to a family unit, it prevents families from focusing on education and forces them into crisis mode.

My mom was a cafeteria worker when I was in elementary school. As you know, not all cafeteria workers are treated very well by teachers, leaders, or students. She worked for a few hours a day and spent the rest of the nights at the hospital when my dad was being treated for cancer. After he passed away, she went back to school to get her general equivalency diploma (GED), but I know she never felt as good as those teachers she often had to meet with to discuss the progress of her children.

As I struggled social-emotionally and academically from year to year, I also happened to notice that most adults around me in school had college diplomas, and most of the families of my friends did as well. However, what I also knew is that my mom had to play the part of father to her five children, of which I was the youngest. I struggled a lot. I graduated ranked fourth from last in my high school class and failed out of two community colleges before finding the right cross-country coach and teacher who helped inspire me to get help from the Learning Assistance Center (LAC) at Hudson Valley Community College in Troy, New York. I then went on to get a bachelor's, two master's degrees, and a doctorate. I had a 4.0 GPA on my last master's and doctorate. I don't write about my GPA to impress; I write about it to show that with the right teachers students can make well over a year's growth for a year's input.

What does that have to do with my perspective on families? As a teacher who spent time in several city schools, I saw families who assumed I cruised through school and came from a family who put me through college; they treated me as though I didn't understand them. What they soon found out is that I understood their issues better than most. At face value, it's easy to judge the families who care too much or care too little, but we never really know what is going on in their heads that drives their behavior. The Meet, Model, and Motivate framework is just as important for families as it is for students and teachers.

The role schools play in life with families is a complicated one. Our school communities are filled with families who believe they know more than we, which may be very true. Our school communities also have families who will support everything we do—typically the families we like the most. On the other end of the spectrum are families who do not trust anything we do, and there may be some good reasons why they don't.

What Do We Expect From Families?

According to the Harvard Family Research Project, "Family, school, and community engagement in education should be an essential strategy in building a pathway to college and career readiness in today's competitive global society" (Weiss, Lopez, & Rosenberg, 2010, p. 1). However, our expectations of families are based on the Goldilocks principle, which is not being too soft, not being too hard, but finding the right balance. This is not easy because every parent we work with seems to have a different expectation of us as educators, at the same time every educator in our school seems to have different expectations of families. Some want families to volunteer while others want families to sign agendas when they go home every night. There are teachers who want families to sit side by side with their children while they do their homework, and other teachers who want their children to do their homework on their own.

As we go up in grade level from elementary to middle and then high school, we want families to take a gradual release of responsibility with their children so those children become empowered instead of enabled, but when that happens, are we really sure they understand what is happening in school? Do we think that is important? We should because we don't often know how well we communicate until a negative situation happens, and families come knocking on our door. To proactively communicate with parents, try handing the following form out at a PTA/O meeting and having a discussion around it. Sometimes parents do not know how to be educationally supportive in the K–12 experience because it's the first child, and they are learning as they go.

Helpful Tips

Tips to Help Build Parental Involvement

Number One: Allow your children to complete tasks on their own. Children should . . .

- Pick up their bedroom.
- Have chores they need to be responsible for, such as taking out the garbage or helping with dishes.
- Work out their problems on their own first. If they still need help after that, then intervene.
- Do their homework on their own. If they have homework, make sure they follow through on the responsibility.
- Check their homework after they're done (however, if they are really having a hard time with it, then intervene).
- If they decide not to complete their homework, let them deal with the consequences at school. They may not make the same mistake twice.

Number Two: Praise your children when they show responsibility.

- Statistic: For every one positive comment, a child hears 10 negative ones.
- Children can never hear that you love them enough. Let them know it every day.
- There is no need to buy them a gift for completing a chore. A nice compliment is enough.

Number Three: Take advantage of teachable moments with your children.

- When children neglect a responsibility, it's a perfect time to teach them about responsibility when they make mistakes.
- Help children find different coping skills for when they make mistakes. Coping skills will help them the next time they run into a problem (e.g., taking a supervised walk when they are angry, writing a list of pros and cons, talking their feelings out with an adult).

Number Four: You're the role model.

- No one makes a larger impact on their children than their parents.
- Spend some quality time with your children because that is what they really want from you.

Recently on Facebook, I asked my friends who were teachers and leaders, as well as my friends who have families and are not in the field of education, to answer my questions: I wanted to know what those educators expect from families and what the families expect from school. The following are some of the responses.

Ashleigh Owira wrote,

I feel like a lot of teachers hold back communicating because some families are resistant to the teacher's feedback. Families need to realize each teacher has a different style, and families should keep an open mind to that. We try to support and teach Tevyn (4th grade), Jilyse (kindergarten), and Traesyn (3 years old) as much at home as we are capable of, in hopes that it will advance them in school and encourage them to challenge themselves in school. Do we want to see hours of homework a night? No way! They need some free time after school to be kids, but we want them to be as far ahead in school as they can.

Teacher leader and parent Joanna Pendergast wrote,

Since we have their young children seven+ hours a day (or more), five days a week, I feel it is imperative to communicate what's going on at home, just as we would communicate what's going on in the classroom. Up all night because of a bad dream? Tell me. The family goldfish died? Tell me. Mom is leaving on a business trip for two weeks? Tell me. Even personal information that you feel may be a factor in the behavior of your child. We can't help our students unless we can get into their worlds. I feel like an open and friendly relationship makes the teacher approachable and also makes those tough conversations easier to have when there is a level of trust and "friendship" between families and teachers.

Vicky Koumbis Cox wrote,

Having a seventh grader who has always had academic opportunities and a fifth grader who has high-functioning autism . . . I prefer open communication. I thankfully have had teachers who have been open to me, e-mailing with any concerns. I like them to be in the loop, especially with my fifth grader . . . if there was a bad morning . . . etcetera so they know HOW he may show up. They also keep me in the loop. I have always felt like it was a team with their teachers. And I like it . . . and I think I would feel very overwhelmed IF it wasn't like this. I am NOT a hoverer, though. I don't question grades unless I see a disconnect with what we have been seeing prior.

High school teacher and parent Jennifer Smithers Marten wrote,

> As a parent, I want a phone call over an online grading system. I want to know that the teachers know my kids as the great people they are, not just a data point. I love when teachers know their interests and share those kinds of things with me.

> As a teacher, I want families to know I know their kids, and I want us to be on the same team. When I was in the classroom, I asked families what they wanted from me and the best way to connect with them. I don't judge the level of involvement—stopped doing that years ago when I realized that all families value education but not all in the same way.

High school teacher and parent Tammy Dingman Johnson wrote,

> We want families involved and then complain when they are. We want them to volunteer but not question. My elementary and middle school children want me involved. My junior in high school often begs me not to be! As a high school teacher, I try to connect with families when they can . . . no judgment. We call, text, e-mail. Often if they feel you truly care and are not calling to judge or complain, you can form a partnership that helps to support and encourage students' success.

One possible solution to understanding family engagement is to have a faculty meeting discussion with teachers and staff, or a series of them, around expectations of families. However, that can lead to a very one-sided discussion, so it's important for teachers and leaders to send out a questionnaire to families, asking them what their expectation is of schools. The reasoning for having this conversation over two faculty meetings is that staff can come to a unified idea of their expectations, and the second meeting can be used to discuss the responses by families. Leaders can even take the responses by families and teachers, find a common theme, and communicate that common theme back to the school community. Instead of calling it an *expectation*, I would call it a *family engagement goal*, which is much friendlier language.

Long Island middle school principal Dennis Schug offers the following 15 ways to have better communication with families.

Communication Is the Key!

Here are 15 ways we encourage the school–home connection.

Source: Courtesy of Dennis Schug.

1. Connect with your child's teachers (share which form of communication works best for you).

2. Call us directly here at HBMS.

3. E-mail us.

4. Register for the parent portal.

5. Sign on for our Remind text messages.

6. Subscribe to PTO PEX (Parent Express) Blasts.

7. Come visit us . . . right here at school!

8. Watch the marquee for updates!

9. Listen for School Messenger calls.

10. Visit our website.

11. Use Twitter to follow the learning that's happening.

12. Follow our schools on Facebook—follow the link from the website to get there.

13. Keep an eye out for school surveys—we use these to find out how we can serve you better!

14. Get to know other families of middle school students . . . join the PTO!

15. Talk with your adolescent (*yes, I am serious*).

We are looking forward to taking this Great Journey . . . **TOGETHER!**

Family Engagement Communication

The reason why family engagement goals are so complicated is that our communication in the past may have sent a very direct message. Taking the Collaborative Leadership Framework into consideration, those four different types of leadership styles can be applied to the ways we communicate as a school community. The following examples provide a better understanding of how the framework for leadership can be used for our communication.

> **Collaborative communication:** We build collective effi-cacy together. We flip communication before meetings. We have parent reps on our committees.
>
> **Negotiation communication:** We care what you say but want you to agree with us.
>
> **Regulation communication:** This is what you need to know.
>
> **Bystander communication:** We will wait until you have an issue before we engage with you.

This may surprise you, but this is an area in which Tim Cooper and his team struggles. They cannot seem to get their feet under them when it comes to parent communication, and he often feels the pressure. Tim often finds himself in the bystander communication mode because he waits for parents to come to him. After all, he is dealing with students who may have recently been hospitalized or incarcerated, and on the other side, he has parents who want to talk with him about changing their child's grades in a class because they need a higher GPA to get into the schools that they want. Of all the areas Tim and his team are deciding to work on for the colla-borative growth improvement cycle, Tim is beginning to real-ize that parent engagement is the area.

Contrary to popular belief, this is an area in which Trudy Cowen excels. She makes sure her teachers communicate extensively with parents and even asks for copies of their cor-respondence. All of the teachers at Eagle Elementary School are required to have Remind accounts set up with parents, and Trudy is on the receiving end of every communication. She wants to make sure she is prepared when she talks with par-ents and spends a great deal of her time crafting newsletters that provide evidence that she is involved in all of the commu-nication that teachers send out. Parents know that when they go to talk with Dr. Cowen that she will have the answers and helps alleviate any tension that happens between parents and the teacher.

Truth be told, as a school principal I always believed that I was a collaborative communicator, but I was not. Most of the communication we sent out was one-sided. We told families what we thought they needed to know, and then we communicated all of the positive things happening in our school. After some time, I realized that I floated between negotiation and regulation communication. Then, I began flipping my parent communication. One morning a few days before our open house I had an idea to create a five-minute video focusing on the Common Core State Standards (CCSS), which were very new to the state of New York where I live, and the Dignity for All Students Act (DASA), which was our antibullying legislation. Writing a narrative in Word and then cutting and pasting it into an e-mail in Edline (parent portal), I explained why I was flipping some communication. I asked families to watch it and respond to me through e-mail if they had questions, or better yet, hold the questions until the open house when we had a designated time to spend with each other before they went to teachers' classrooms. Within 30 minutes, I started hearing from families who loved it, and our open house was standing room only. We didn't talk as much about the CCSS, but we did talk about bullying.

I have written about that night before because it had a profound impact on me as a leader, but what I haven't really written about is that the lessons families taught me did not end there. Over time, I realized our newsletters and classroom communication sent a very hidden message that we didn't all see, but families did. We sent home newsletters that highlighted families who could volunteer on a regular basis, which made the families who worked one, two, or three jobs feel bad because they could never volunteer. After that, I made sure the communication I flipped engaged families in a different way. I made sure that we highlighted the everyday life of our students and that we were a professional development school for a local university. Additionally, I tried thinking of our communication in our families' perspective. What did they need to know about their child's educational experience? What could I flip that would offer them something to talk about at the dinner table with their children?

Stop. Collaborate and Listen!

- Think of one idea you could flip to families.
- Write a short narrative to families about the flipped communication process.
- Create a video using social media tools such as Touchcast, which is a free app on your tablet.
- If you can do it before an open house, flip a video focusing on a topic you will talk with families about at the event.
- Create a short video about the day in the life of students in your school. Make sure you have parent permission to use pictures of their children.
- Send the video out through your parent portal or through social media like Twitter and Facebook.
- Don't schedule your flipped communication because if you tell families you will flip every Friday and miss a Friday, it seems as though you're not committed.

The National PTA created six standards for schools to consider when working with families. Those six standards are as follows:

- Welcoming all families into the school community
- Communicating effectively
- Supporting student success
- Speaking up for every child
- Sharing power
- Collaborating with the community

Even with these six standards in mind, sometimes leaders and teachers are content with their communication because they send something out that families can read, but they're not always sure families are reading it. Additionally, they may be sending out communication that creates a disconnection with some families because the images focus on all the families who attended the event and leave out the fact that some families just cannot make it to school. What does your communication look like? Is it authentic or compliant? Even though schools have numerous ways to communicate, the fact is that many teachers and leaders haven't improved on it.

Earlier in this chapter, I provided some great comments that appeared on my Facebook page after I asked about the expectations of families. However, there were other comments that highlighted the expectations some teachers and leaders have for their families. One person wrote,

> As a teacher in a low-income (70% free/reduced lunch) elementary school, I expect nothing. We teach as if they aren't getting much support at home and find older students to read with them and TAs to reteach things that would normally be done for homework.

What was interesting about the comment is that this person followed up by writing,

> As a parent of two kindergarten students, a third grader and an 11th grader, I love lots of communication! I am happy to support the school/teachers any way that I can. Last year, my daughter was in second grade, and I think her teacher expected a little too much to be learned at home. As much as I wanted to support her, she was often extremely tired after school and had a very hard time learning new concepts (in math) at night.

Stop. Collaborate and Listen!

- Use SurveyMonkey to create a survey for teachers and families to gain an understanding of their expectations of each other. Use one survey for families and one for teachers.
- One the most frustrating issues for people completing a survey is when they don't see any changes based on the responses they offered. It's hard to make a lot of changes, but at least send the results to parents to show transparency.
- If leaders can, they should try to find a common theme that may be an issue and make an improvement there.
- SurveyMonkey has preestablished family engagement surveys; see below for a sample of the questions they offer. If leaders don't want to create their own, they can use one that SurveyMonkey has already created (https://www.surveymonkey.com/mp/harvard-education-surveys).

K–12 Parent Survey

In this survey, we are interested in learning more about your thoughts, feelings, and attitudes towards your child's school.

When answering these questions, please consider your child's current experience at school. This survey is to help us understand different aspects of the parent/school relationship. Your answers will be used in aggregate, and we will not be evaluating individual responses. As such, please be as honest as possible—there are no right or wrong answers.

Because different children often have different experiences in the same school, please complete this survey once per child.

1. Please write only the FIRST name of your child who is attending your school. _____

In this first section, we'd like to learn more about some of your roles, beliefs, and attitudes as well as some of the activities that you do as the parent of a school-aged child.

2. How often do you meet in person with teachers at your child's school?

   ☐ Almost never

   ☐ Once or twice per year

   ☐ Every few months

   ☐ Monthly

   ☐ Weekly or more

3. How confident are you that you can help your child develop good friendships?

   ☐ Not confident at all

   ☐ Slightly confident

   ☐ Somewhat confident

   ☐ Quite confident

   ☐ Extremely confident

(Other questions include the following.)

4. How much effort do you put into helping your child learn to do things for himself/herself?

9. How confident are you in your ability to make sure your child's school meets your child's learning needs?

13. To what extent do you know how your child is doing socially at school?

(Continued)

(Continued)

14. How confident are you in your ability to help your child deal with his or her emotions appropriately?

15. Do you have any comments about any of your answers to the questions in this section?

In this section, we'd like to learn more about your perceptions of your child and your child's interactions with his or her school.

17. On average, how well does your child work independently on learning activities at home?

19. At your child's school, how well does the overall approach to discipline work for your child?

20. How much effort does your child put into school related tasks?

21. How much of a sense of belonging does your child feel at his or her school?

24. In general, how well does your child learn from feedback about his or her work?

In this section, we'd like to learn more about your perceptions of the overall climate at your child's school.

26. To what extent do you think that children enjoy going to your child's school?

28. How motivating are the classroom lessons at your child's school?

29. How well do administrators at your child's school create a school environment that helps children learn?

30. Overall, how much respect do you think the teachers at your child's school have for the children?

Source: https://www.surveymonkey.com/mp/harvard-education-surveys. Copyright © 1999–2017 SurveyMonkey.

Do we lower our expectations just because of the bank account, or lack thereof, of our families? Have we really tried to engage them? Do we use too much edu-speak with them when they do meet with us? There are many times when families living in poverty do come to school early on and want to be engaged, but our low expectations and the way we talk with them lead to a disconnection.

Hattie (2009) writes, "Schooling introduces a language and set of cultural norms with which many families, particularly those from lower SES families, are not familiar" (p. 63). Additionally, Clinton, Hattie, and Dixon (2007) found major consequences when teaching families the language of schooling. This research comes from the Flaxmere Project, which was a five-year, five-school study completed in New Zealand that included the lowest SES (socioeconomic status) schools in the country. According to Hattie, "The Flaxmere Project involved a series of innovations related to improving home–school relations within and between these five schools" (2009, p. 63). One of the innovations was to hire former teachers as home–school liaisons, and those liaisons taught families the language of schooling, how to assist their children to attend and engage in learning, and how to speak with teachers and school personnel. Hattie found the following:

> The Flaxmere study found that, when children started school, 98% of the families considered that education was very or extremely important to their children's future. Two-thirds of these families expected their children to attain diplomas and degrees. (2009, p. 63)

However, what Clinton and colleagues (2007) found was that "by the time they left elementary school, these aspirations had been dowsed and families mainly wanted their children to get a job" (Hattie, 2009, p. 70).

Instead of blaming parents for not being engaged, we should ask why they aren't and see if our communication contributes to that lack of involvement. The Harvard Family

Research Study reported on by Wesiss and colleagues (2010) suggests,

> Through data sharing, school districts and schools are responsible for communicating student perfor-mance with families. Beyond providing access to data, schools also provide training and assistance to ensure that families grasp the meaning of the data so that they can partner with teachers to take action and support a student's learning goals. (p. 11)

Schools can meet this need by offering family engagement nights once a month. Instead of offering the old run-of-the-mill PTA/O meetings, school leaders can ask teachers to donate their time on a rotating basis to teach parents the important aspects of data. Therefore, by the time parents attend parent–teacher conferences, they are better equipped to be a part of the data and report conversations with teachers. Clearly, this would take time to plan what each month would look like and which data are most important. Additionally, it would mean that the executive committee of the PTA/O would have to come in an hour early to go over the executive aspects of the PTA/O group.

I saw a great example of data sharing the first time I visited New Zealand. On a school visit to the Silvia Park School in the Mt. Wellington section of Auckland, I was introduced to their data coach. As we sat down to discuss her job, she told me that a part of her duties was to meet parents on their lunch breaks to go over their child's growth data. She actually drove to the workplace of the parent to meet over the parent's lunch break. When I asked how teachers felt about it, she said, "It's not the teacher's data. We all own it." This data sharing became part of their school culture and created a climate in which parents felt as if they were partners in their child's learning.

Unfortunately, many teachers and leaders will not try to do either of these family engagement methods because they prefer compliant engagement in which parents don't ask a lot of questions. Understanding our expectations of parents and looking at our own communication with them is an important step in the process. Do we want authentic engagement or compliant engagement when it comes to parents?

Is Your Parent Engagement Authentic or Compliant?

Peter DeWitt (2016b)

June 14, 2016
Finding Common Ground Blog—blogs.edweek.org

Newsletters . . . *check.*

Open house . . . *check.*

Parent–teacher conferences . . . *check.*

Flipping parent communication . . . *check.*

Branding . . . *check.*

School leaders and teachers often try to build parental involvement. They make pretty newsletters, flip their communication, and brand their message out to families so that families know what's going on in their child's school. These approaches, all of which I did as a school principal, are a much better way to communicate with families than what our families had when we were students.

Unfortunately, how those tools are used is an important part of whether the parental involvement we are trying to increase is authentic or compliant. Yes, there is a difference. Authentic engagement happens when families can have real dialogue with teachers and leaders—even if that dialogue means that all parties don't start the conversation agreeing with each other.

(Continued)

(Continued)

Compliant engagement means that school leaders and teachers send the message, and families have to *support* those two parties at home. It means that families, teachers, and leaders form a unified front to the students when they're in school and when they're home, which is another way of expecting compliance from children at school and at home.

I remember a parent told me that when her children were giving her a hard time at Wal-Mart, she would say, "Was that Dr. DeWitt I saw around the corner? You don't want him to see you acting like this, do you?" I laughed, and then I found myself instantly mortified because I didn't want the children to think I played the part of disciplinarian in all parts of my job. I felt a bit like I played second fiddle to Elf on the Shelf.

We all have our roles in the school community, but we should be allowed to update those roles.

Engage Every Parent?

In *Engage Every Family: Five Simple Principles* (Constantino, 2016), superintendent and consultant Steve Constantino outlines five principles that every school adheres to where family engagement is concerned. Those five principles are as follows:

A culture that engages every family: Constantino writes, "The collective beliefs, attitudes, norms, values, actions, and assumptions of the school organization explicitly embrace and are committed to the notion of families as a foundational core component to improvement" (p. 52). He delves into the cultures and subcultures that exist within schools. Constantino says that we all have certain cycles within our schools that need to be broken because they affect our cultures negatively.

Communicate effectively and build relationships: Constantino starts out with suggestions such as staff trainings, community outreach programs, and family week. We know that communicating effectively and building relationships is important, but Constantino points out that sometimes the first messages that our families see when they arrive at school aren't all that friendly. Think about it . . . they see signs like "Faculty/Staff Parking Only," and "Warning!

Trespassers Will Be Prosecuted!" In these days of increased security, we have to find a way to soften our message a little.

Empower every family: In order to empower every family, Constantino writes that we should believe that "families are recognized as essential members of the learning team for each student—their participation is welcomed, valued, and encouraged by the school" (p. 128).

Engage every family in decision-making: We need to include families in the decision-making process at school. One of the most effective ways to include families in the decision-making process is through stakeholder groups—where the decision isn't already made before the group is formed. Families must have an authentic voice in the school community.

Engage the greater community: Constantino focuses on community schools. In the book, he writes, "A community school is both a place and a set of partnerships where an integrated focus on academics, services, supports, and opportunities leads to improved student learning, stronger families, and healthier communities" (p. 179).

Many Hands Make Light Work

When I began my principalship in 2006, I was charged with working with a large group of families to design and build the playground for our school. Sound easy? It's a playground, right? Not really. Our school was on 26 acres, and the structure that was wanted was somewhere between something small that would blend into the natural setting and a Six Flags for the community. After all, in a rural community the school is the center where everyone comes together.

Over the next few months, we all worked together to design a structure that was a good balance between blending in and the Six Flags some wanted. As much as there was a great deal of back and forth between families and committee members, the best part of designing the playground was when we came together over a weekend to build it.

There were a few families who were engineers and business owners that took the lead, and the rest of us did the grunt work, and it was one of the best experiences I had as a principal. The playground structure was a symbol of the importance of school staff and families working together.

(Continued)

> (Continued)
>
> **In the End**
>
> Families are important. We know that. Not just because they send their children to us on a daily basis, but because many of them become friends and provide us with important insight. We have gone through happy times with them and held their hands during very tough times. A lot of life happens in our time in schools, and families are right there with us when it all takes place.
>
> Give Constantino's book a deep read because he offers some important tips that you, as leaders and teachers, may not be doing yet. Steve has been at the forefront of parent engagement for many decades, and his words may just help you bond a little more with those families you've been having a difficult time reaching.

Understanding whether we want authentic or compliant engagement on the part of parents is an important discussion. We cannot complain that they aren't there to support their children if we hold our hands up, stopping them from coming in when they want to discuss a topic with us. The back-and-forth dialogue are all a part of family engagement. According to the Harvard Family Research Project, there are three key elements of family engagement:

- Family engagement is a shared responsibility.
- Family engagement is continuous across a child's life.
- Family engagement cuts across and reinforces learning in the multiple settings where children learn. (Weiss et al., 2010, p. 11)

It's interesting because we have hundreds of ways to communicate and work through those three important elements of family engagement, but the increased volume of the possible tools doesn't mean we communicate any better. What we have to do is understand why we are communicating in the first place. Leaders and teachers need to ask parents what they expect out of the communication from school, and those leaders and teachers may end up finding out important information from parents, as long as those teachers and leaders are open to listening.

Do We Openly Listen to Families?

The following list about how to become a better listener is not just about how leaders work with families, but how they work with everyone in the school community. However, it seems to be a good place to focus on listening because it's easy to judge families for the choices they make and not really listen to them when they are standing in front of us. Parent–leader conversations can sometimes be escalated based on the situation they are talking about, and in that case, leaders need to really think about Covey's (1989) thought: "Most people do not listen with the intent to understand; they listen with the intent to reply."

Recently, I came across a powerful TED Talk, *Ten Ways to Have a Better Conversation*, by NPR host Celeste Headlee. Those ten suggestions, along with my explanations, appear in the list Ten Ways to Become a Better Listener.

Ten Ways to Become a Better Listener

1. **Don't multitask:** It's rude and sends the message that we're not listening fully.

2. **Don't pontificate:** We need to get off our soapbox. When we pontificate, it seems as though we think we are right every time. No need to have a conversation if we're not opening to learning while we're in it.

3. **Use open-ended questions:** Ask questions that will inspire the other person to share their whole story, so we can get to the bottom of the issue.

(Continued)

(Continued)

4. **Go with the flow:** Sometimes we want to make sure we say what we are thinking, even if that means we half-listen to retain our own thoughts. If what we're thinking is so vital, we will remember it when they are done speaking. Better yet, their thoughts may inspire us to think of something better.

5. **If you don't know, say you don't know:** Don't fake it. We need to act as though we are on record and what we say will be held against us. If we don't know, we should just admit we don't know.

6. **Don't equate your experiences with theirs:** This one is a hard one for many of us. Very often, we want to share our experience to build credibility and show the persons speaking that we empathize with them. Headlee says that this makes the conversation about us and not them. We should listen.

7. **Try not to repeat yourself:** When we repeat ourselves over and over again, it may come off as condescending. We really only have to say it once for people to hear it.

8. **Stay out of the weeds:** Headlee said we shouldn't get caught up in dates and times when telling a story. We should stick to the point of the story more than pausing to get the date right.

9. **Listen:** We do not do this enough. We need to listen with the intent to understand. The interesting point Headlee brings up is that our brains are conditioned to speak on average 225 words per minute, but we are conditioned to listen to 500 words a minute, which means our brains are looking for ways to fill in those other 275 words when someone is talking to us.

10. **Be brief:** Have you ever been on the receiving end of someone who talks and talks and talks? We shouldn't do that or we inspire the other person to float off out of our conversation. (Headlee, 2016)

Principal Dennis Schug has spent many years perfecting his communication with parents. In the following vignette, he describes the numerous ways the school tries to communicate, but in one meeting with a parent, he found that after years of using the same letter, the communication he was using was getting lost in translation.

Practitioner's Voice

Does Your Communication Get Lost in Translation?

Dennis Schug, Principal
Hampton Bays Middle School
Long Island, New York

Consistent school–home communication is a cornerstone to student success at Hampton Bays Middle School. As a new middle school principal, I quickly realized the value parents place on feeling their children are safe and thriving as learners. Our middle school learning community works every day to explore communication tools that can nourish a strong 21st century school–home partnership.

Effective communication has been my leadership focus for seven years, and I believe it contributes to a much stronger school climate, and therefore, a stronger school community.

We use traditional options like telephone and e-mail. We also use options that have two-way potential, such as our student management system, report cards, and social media platforms, including a school Twitter account and a district Facebook account. Additionally, there are tools that provide timely information, including moderate tech-based options such as our automated telephone system, texting and e-mail blast services, and a school website.

At Hampton Bays, we keep our roadside message board and parent–teacher organizations for parents who find comfort in more traditional approaches. Regular letters and memos from the principal and notes, specific to classrooms, grade levels, teams, and departments round out our menu, and all are aimed at connecting educators at school with parents at home.

(Continued)

(Continued)

Overall, we promote over 15 means of communication, excluding tools, virtual classroom spaces, and shared calendars being piloted or used by our teachers. All parents have to do is select the option that suits their needs and preferences.

By all appearances, we're communicating! However, although we use so many ways to communicate effectively with families, we found out that some of our communication was getting lost in translation. That moment happened at our bilingual parent meeting.

Lost in Translation

DeWitt has his Meet, Model, and Motivate Framework (2016a), and it's something we strive to do with all stakeholders. In an effort to "meet families where they are," our district sponsors meetings for bilingual parents, where we welcome Spanish-speaking families in an open-forum setting. Parents attend, eager to connect with teachers, administrators, and other parents. Specific questions are asked about children and education. Our shared vision is clear: to work together to maximize our shared vision for student success.

During one particular meeting I won't soon forget, a mother shared a form letter that we have sent home several times a year for a number of years. It's written both in English and Spanish. It includes periodic updates to two local classroom-based assessments that our teachers use to measure each student's individual academic progress and to inform their teaching practices. These letters are intended as progress indicators.

During this bilingual parent meeting, I came to learn several things. The words *quantile* and *lexile* do not translate well to Spanish. They present parents with obstacles, leaving them to either navigate "teacher-talk" in print or dismiss our flawed communication altogether. This runs a risk of parents feeling alienated, avoiding school, and it eliminates opportunities for correspondence between teachers and parents to exchange feedback and set student achievement goals together.

The bottom of this letter bears my signature.

First, I blushed. Then, I sat with this parent and invited our bilingual facilitator over to join us. My apology was met with a forgiving smile. Together, we adjusted the verbiage so that moving forward, the letter can serve as it is intended, an effective school–home outreach. I realized then what I often profess to anyone willing to listen: Any tool is a potential *conversation starter.*

The best communication, however, happens *face-to-face.* We just have to be open to listening.

In the End

If we want our families to be engaged, we need to have school climates that engage them, which means we have to understand that our students have families who have blended families and are straight or gay. Do we make all of them feel welcome? Additionally, I know it seems politically correct to say family engagement instead of parental involvement, but not all family units are traditional families. They may have grandparents, foster families, aunts and uncles, or some children who are raised by an older sibling. The reason why this is important is it helps us understand that we have to meet them where they are and not where we expect them to be when they come to our schools. Children who are growing up in families that do not look representative of the family image that comes up in our mind need to have images, books, and curriculum that are representative of them.

In this chapter, we learned from leaders and teachers like Dennis Schug and Jennifer Smithers Marten, who told us how they engage families and how they learned from some mistakes they made. Martin and Schug both have the qualities necessary to engage in the better conversations that Headlee suggests in her powerful TED Talk. I think the story Dennis wrote about is powerful because many leaders may not have noticed that the letter was written in edu-speak and would have felt that writing the letter in Spanish was good enough.

It all begins with understanding the expectations we have of families but also understanding the expectations they have of us. Collaborative leaders who want to create a more positive school climate put out surveys or questionnaires, asking families what their hopes and dreams are for their children. And then they make sure that the school community is one that helps keep those hopes and dreams alive. That doesn't happen through lowering our expectations, like that of the teacher who posted the earlier comment on my Facebook page when I asked about expectations of families. It doesn't happen when we use educational acronyms they cannot understand, which is why Dennis Schug's vignette is so important.

So, as we already know, if we want to reach the students, we also have to make an effort to reach families. Perhaps this means getting a home–school liaison to help engage families, but it also means addressing the way we talk with them.

Tips for Engaging Families

Drop the education lingo: We need to either teach the families what the words or acronyms mean (every profession has acronyms), or we have to drop the educational lingo and acronyms to better engage the families.

Adjust expectations: I never really liked the "high expectations" movement because it got too political. However, we do need to focus on helping students exceed the expectations they or their families have for themselves, which means that we do have to have higher expectations for them, regardless of what family they come from. This happens in rural, urban, and suburban settings.

Respect the contributions from home: Home environment has a 0.57 effect size, which means that we have to engage all families, regardless of whether they live in poverty or not. Parental involvement has an effect size of 0.51, so we should make sure that we are talking with them about learning instead of talking at them about behavior. Sometimes, we need to teach the families the language of learning so we are all working together to encourage and help students exceed what they think is their potential.

I'd like to end with one more practical strategy for leaders and teachers to use that will help build collaboration with families. The Student-Led Conferences blog post that follows could easily have appeared in the chapter on students, but this book is about how all of the stakeholders in schools are interrelated, and I believe student-led conferences are just as powerful for families coming into school as they are for students learning within the school.

Student-Led Conferences

Peter DeWitt (2011)

November 1, 2011
Finding Common Ground Blog—blogs.edweek.org

> *We take the mystery out of learning because we have a habit of talking at children and not to them.*

As many schools prepare for parent–teacher conferences, they should consider involving the students in the process. It sounds like a radical concept to involve the students in the process of discussing their academic progress, but it is an approach that many schools use and has been around for decades. It's called *student-led conferences*.

For a long time, schooling has focused on **one to glow on, one to grow on, and one to go on.** During the conference, teachers tell parents an area of strength, an area of weakness, and an area that is improving. If you are a parent, you may feel that conferences are a time when a teacher is telling you what is wrong with your child, which is not the goal of the teacher, but some parents walk into a classroom and are instantly transported back to when they were a kid. Parent–teacher conferences can be very intimidating.

I remember the fear of my mom leaving our house to go meet with my teachers when I was in elementary school. I watched out the living room window as she backed down the driveway. I worried that she may never

(Continued)

(Continued)

return again, or if she did, she would be angry when she walked in the kitchen door. I was fearful because I wasn't sure what she would hear. Was I doing something wrong? Would they only focus on the math tests that I failed? Would the speech teacher attend the meeting and tell my mother that I could not say the *R* sound? If I lived in Massachusetts, my *R* would sound fine!

The truth is, to children the idea of their parent meeting with the teacher is a frightening experience. Children still think that teachers and the principal live at school, and they are surprised when they run into us at the mall or the grocery store. So when their parent meets with the teacher, students worry about the conversation because they know it is all about them.

Parent–Teacher Conferences Have Not Changed for Decades

In the past, students were left out of the conference because teachers and parents were trying to watch out for the self-esteem of the children. It was easier to talk about their improvement needs if they weren't present. In addition, it was not considered important to have the students present for the conference.

As adults, we do a very good job of telling children what they need to do differently. We do not always do a good job of asking them what they think they need to do differently. We take the mystery out of learning because we have a habit of talking at children and not to them.

However, there has always been one flaw with leaving students out of the conference, which is that they know what they can and cannot do. Telling children who can't read well that they cannot read well is something they already know because they listen to their peers read and understand they have a weakness in reading. We can change the names of the groups to reflect happy animals, such as Lions, Tigers, and Bears, but children know that the Bears are the great readers!

One other reason that conferences tend to be the same as they have been for the past few decades is that the teachers are under time constraints. They have one day or maybe one night and a full day to meet with 27 parents. Collecting all of the data that needs to be discussed as well as making sure that the meeting starts and ends on time is stressful.

The key to any successful meeting between parents, children, and teachers is time management and organization. It takes a great deal of proactive work to make sure that everyone is set for a student-led conference.

How Do Student-Led Conferences Work?

Preparing for student-led conferences really begins at the beginning of the school year. As the quarter or trimester goes on, students begin collecting their favorite pieces of work and add them to a portfolio. More technologically advanced schools may incorporate online portfolios instead of hard copies in folders.

Great writing assignments, art projects, or anything that focuses on the strength of a child can be added to a portfolio to be used during a student-led conference. Depending on the age, children need to know what makes a good addition to their portfolio because they may want to add everything they do, which would be overwhelming.

As the conference time approaches, the teacher spends time with the class discussing what the best pieces would be to include in their portfolios. Students decorate their portfolio and add a table of contents so that everyone who views the portfolio knows what is in it.

During the conference time, the teacher usually sets up a 30 to 40 minute conference with the parents. The first 15 to 20 minutes of the conference are between the child and her or his parent. Parents sit in a designated spot with their child, and they are led through the portfolio. This is an important time for parents to have questions for their children and be fully engaged in the process. When parents can't attend or do not show up for the conference, perhaps another teacher (librarian, reading teacher, music teacher, etc.) or the principal can meet with the child during a nonconference day to go through the portfolio.

After the parent and child work through the portfolio, the teacher meets with the child and parent. The teacher may discuss the portfolio and talk with the parent about the work that was good, as well as about areas in which the child can improve. The purpose of the conference is to provide children with a full picture of how they are doing in class. It helps to build maturity with the student as well as give them an opportunity to discuss their own learning.

(Continued)

(Continued)

Student-led conferences need to be done in an age-appropriate way. K–2 students could choose the work that is included in their portfolios but might not be able to lead a conference with their parents. Students in third grade and above are certainly capable of leading their parents through a conference.

In the End

In order to properly engage students in their own learning, we must allow them the opportunity to be a part of the conference between a teacher and parent. Allowing them to choose their own pieces for a portfolio adds to the concept that the child is the center of the learning process.

As students get older, they are at risk to become less engaged in school, and student-led conferences allow them to be fully engaged in the process. It also helps parents communicate better with their children and perhaps can even help parents feel more engaged in their child's academic progress as well.

Student-led conferences may be something that teachers cannot do presently because of time constraints, but they could consider doing it in the future. It would make for a great goal for a spring conference or the next school year. The time devoted to student-led conferences is time well spent.

ACTION STEPS

- Talk with faculty about their expectations of families.
- Survey your families to ask about their expectations of school.
- What is your current reality when it comes to your communication?
  - Are you a negotiator, bystander, or regulator?
- Use Dennis Schug's 15 Ways to Communicate.
- Watch Celeste Headlee's engaging Ted Talk.

DISCUSSION QUESTIONS

- How do you survey teachers about their expectations of families? What do they say?
- How have you created family stakeholder groups or surveyed families to ask them what their expectations are of school?
- What have been some of the best ways you have used to engage families?
    - How do you know you were successful?
    - What could you do differently?

TIM AND TRUDY

- Did anything surprise you about Tim and Trudy's family engagement?
- Where do you believe Tim should start when it comes to his family engagement goal?
- How could Trudy take her family engagement strength and use it in her other leadership practices?
- Is there anything Tim and Trudy can learn from each other where family engagement is concerned?

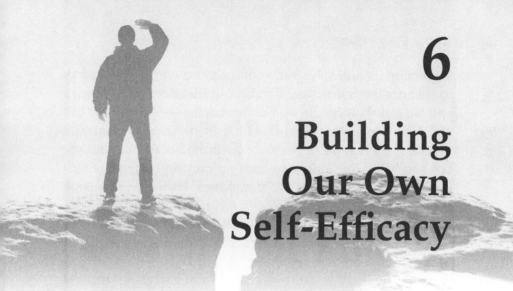

6

Building
Our Own
Self-Efficacy

*Just because you're stuck with their policy, doesn't mean you
need to be stuck with their mindset.*

—Michael Fullan

A Tale of Two Leaders

Let's close out our story with Trudy Cowen and Tim Cooper. As the book unfolded, you learned a little bit more about their strengths and weaknesses, as well as their mindsets. The mindset we have as leaders is really important because it doesn't affect just us—it has an effect on everyone around us. When we walk down the hallway and smile or engage with a student, teacher, staff member, or family member, those individuals walk away from us either feeling as though we care or they walk away feeling as if we don't have an understanding one way or another. When that happens, we miss a point of impact.

Every time we engage with a person we have the opportunity to build a bridge or construct a wall. Collaborative leadership is about constantly building bridges. Collaborative leadership includes the purposeful actions we take as leaders to enhance the instruction of teachers, build deep relationships with all stakeholders through understanding self-efficacy (0.63), and build collective efficacy (1.57) to deepen our learning together. There have been examples provided throughout the book to help you understand self-efficacy and collective efficacy, as well as how to raise it in others. However, this book is not just about leaders. Whether you're an aspiring leader or want to stay in the classroom, our self-efficacy and how we contribute to collective efficacy matters. Everyone has an important role in the classroom.

Unfortunately, in our two examples of leadership that we began with, one of the leaders did not take the time to understand self-efficacy or collective efficacy. In the long run, Trudy found out that her insecurities in being a leader got the best of her. Instead of instilling her trust into her staff, she spent day after day pummeling them with compliance measures that did not result in better test scores and certainly did not result in a more positive and inclusive school climate.

In fact, in her second year the school had a holiday party, as schools do around Christmas and Hanukah, and the attendance rate was less than half from the year before. For Trudy, that was less a sign that she had to change her leadership style and more of a sign that she needed to tighten the reins because the staff was unsupportive. On her return from the holidays, she once again checked lesson plans and never provided feedback, and with her three untenured teachers, she made them hand in every lesson plan they created for each day to the point that they quit teaching by the end of the year.

Dr. Andrea Norton, the school superintendent, worked hard to get Trudy a mentor over the years, but she wouldn't take any of the advice given. Professional development became more about compliance, and teachers were required to hand in proof of learning, which took them away from focusing on the learning of their students. School events like diversity days were turned into competitions among teachers, and Trudy would celebrate the hard work of those who supported her and chastise the work of those who were, in her mind, against her.

Families—a group that she did well with from the beginning—began to hear from their children that she was not kind in the hallway, and they soon found that the teachers felt the same way. The Eagle Elementary School community was fractured, and they began complaining to the superintendent because the two other elementary school principals were beloved as much as Trudy was disliked. Unfortunately, the teachers and staff at Eagle Elementary School put in a vote of no confidence, and after a year of fighting, Trudy resigned from her position.

Tim Cooper had a very different experience. After a few interactions with families, he went to a few parents he had gotten to know over the years and asked them how he could do a better job of engaging more families. Although a few of the parents said he always did a great job, there were a couple of parents who told Tim some things he could work on. At the top of the list was communication. They remarked about how they did not know that students were being innovative in school, and they also didn't realize that Waterville High School was a professional development school for Sage University, which was a university about 10 minutes away.

Tim began flipping his family communication. He would go through classes taking pictures and tweeting them out. He used the hashtag #watervillehigh in all of his tweets and promoted the use of Twitter on the school website. Tim even started sending short videos and pictures of students with a short narrative through Edline, their parent portal page. Edline had been used mostly for parents to keep up on the grades of their students, but only about 45 percent of families were actively using it. As Tim began tweeting and sending out videos through flipped communication, more and more families signed up, and by the end of the year, Tim had moved up to having 78 percent of the parents signed on, and then at the beginning of the next year, it moved up to 85 percent because he promoted it at the open house.

Even the open house was different because Tim flipped out a video three days ahead of the event, inviting families and telling them that he planned on sharing some of the innovative learning tools they were using at school, and he recruited a few students from each grade level to explain each one.

Tim soon found that flipping his communication before open house worked because he had standing room only. He still had some parents to get to, but he found that all of the adults had a smartphone, so they all had access to a tool with which they could read newsletters and view videos.

At the end of the first year and then the second year of his communication blitz to parents, Tim put out a survey asking the families how he could communicate better, and to his surprise, the unanimous answer was that he was communicating effectively, and they wanted him to continue to use the same ways. The school climate at Waterville High School was one of pride, where families felt as welcome as Tim had already made his teachers and students feel. It wasn't perfect and still needed work, but he was willing to work with his team to become even more effective.

The sad part for Tim was that Dr. Norton would ask him to talk about his innovations with family engagement and school climate at administration meetings, and he noticed that Trudy always had a reason why she couldn't implement them. He offered to help her a few times, but she said she was doing just fine, thanking him for the offer. In the end, Tim realized that he wished he had tried a little harder to connect with Trudy.

Focus on Strengths and One Weakness

- What are your strengths? How do you maximize them?
- How do you feel about your own level of self-efficacy?
- What is one weakness you would like to work on?
- Who can you enlist to help you?

What's Your Mindset?

Mindset is a word we hear a lot. There is a growth mindset, an innovator's mindset, and I've written about a collaborative mindset. Changing our mindset is not always easy in leadership and teaching. We all get caught up in doing what we've always done because it makes us feel good—especially when we are bombarded with so many mandates and tasks to complete each day. By the time we consider our mindsets, the day may be already done, and we are driving home, reflecting on the day.

Leaders have a lot to worry about. They worry about the home lives of their students and the social-emotional health of all stakeholders in the school community. Leaders are often in the position of hearing the best and worst from parents, students, and staff. As a school principal, I was often happy that parents wanted to engage with me, but I found myself profoundly sad from the stories they told. I will never ever forget sitting with parents the day after they found out their child was terminally ill.

I have been through school consolidations, budget votes, state police at board meetings, countless calls to Child Protective Services (CPS), active shooter drills, students having seizures that had gone undiagnosed, and deaths of former staff members and students. I know that is not uplifting, but it is the reality of a school leader, as well as anyone else who works in a school. As we know from the words of Bandura (1977, 1986, 1997), those experiences are the ones where we learn a lot about ourselves and they can help increase our self-efficacy.

On the other side, I have had the good fortune of meeting hundreds of great families, been through countless celebrations with them as well as staff, and have seen the growth of thousands of students over the years. Through those relationships and building trust, I knew that I did not have to do it alone. I had many families, teachers, and staff who were willing to help me out on those issues where I struggled.

When it comes to collaborative leadership, what is your mindset? How do you approach the types of situations I described? How do you react when people want to take time to talk with you? When you see students in the hallway, even on your tough days, how do you interact with them? What is your mindset? If you struggle with being more collaborative, look at Figure 6.1 for suggestions how to change your mindset.

As I wrote earlier in this book, the World Health Organization (WHO) predicts that one in four people in the world will be affected by mental or neurological disorders at some point in their lives and that two-thirds of people will never get assistance (WHO, 2001b). This has implications for

Figure 6.1   A Collaborative Mindset

Instead of . . .	Try . . .
Focusing on behavior	Focusing on learning
Demanding answers	Fostering questions
Checking lesson plans of all teachers	Linking teacher autonomy with growth evidence of students (Hattie)
Sending blanket e-mails to staff focusing on compliance	Talking one-on-one with teachers
Patrolling the hallways	Engaging in conversation with students
Using checklists to complete formal observations	Providing feedback focused on a teacher-chosen, student-centered goal (linking together each observation)
Meeting with parents when they have issues	Making learning transparent to parents by flipping, branding, and communicating
Focusing on dates and new mandates in faculty meetings	Flipping faculty meetings to focus on PD teachers need
Reading education books and coming up with new ideas in isolation	Understanding the current reality of your school and collaborating with teachers to find solutions
Building consensus	Building relationships
Talking at students	Talking with students
Being reactive	Being proactive

leaders because those suffering are parents, students, and staff members. And that is why the school climate is so vitally important. Our school climate can be a place that engages more students and families. A positive and supportive school climate fosters the growth of teachers and staff so they can help engage the school community. I strongly believe that a positive and inclusive school climate can be a beacon of hope for many communities.

Clearly, this is not easy. In order for a community to be strong and caring, there needs to be a leader that is strong and caring as well. Unfortunately, very often collaborative leaders care about bringing everyone together, but they put themselves last. In fact, in an informal study of school leaders from a few years ago—conducted by Jerome Murphy, former dean of the Harvard Graduate School—showed that 89 percent reported feeling overwhelmed, 84 percent neglected to take care of themselves in the midst of stress, and 80 percent scolded themselves when they performed less than perfectly (Olsen & Brown, 2012).

In order to be effective, leaders have to remember to do a little self-care from time to time. The point is for leaders to go from always feeling reactive and overwhelmed to being proactive and feeling more confident.

Leading From Within: Mindfulness Practices for School Leaders

Valerie Brown

August 16, 2015
Finding Common Ground Blog—blogs.edweek.org

We are in the midst of a mindfulness revolution in the United States and worldwide. Research-based studies on mindfulness have skyrocketed over

(Continued)

(Continued)

the past 30 years, and mindfulness is now offered within many sectors of American society: schools and colleges, Fortune 200 and Fortune 500 companies, the U.S. military, among major U.S. and international sports teams, and even in the halls of the U.S. Congress. Much of this interest in mindfulness is fueled by research on the workings of the brain, made possible, in part, because of advances in functional MRIs.

There is a neurobiological revolution in the understanding of how the mind, body, and brain work together and function. One of the great scientific revolutions of our time is the stunning advancement in understanding the workings of the human brain over the last three decades. We are rapidly gaining insights into the relationships between what we think and how we perform, see the world, feel, and are prompted to act. To a far greater extent than we've realized, we have influence on of the *shape* of our brains.

Neuroplasticity: The Science Behind Mindfulness

The old assumption was that our brains stopped growing by late childhood and started to decline around age 25. We now know that both of these ideas are wrong.

Neuroplasticity refers to the brain's ability to change its pattern and structure throughout our lifetime, and this highlights a different picture.

Dr. Richard J. Davidson's book, *The Emotional Life of Your Brain*, describes how your experiences, mental activity, thinking, and motivation can affect that change. The brain is shaped by your environment, your experience, and your beliefs; it never stops maturing. The brain possesses the capacity for lifelong neuroplasticity. For school leaders, this means that the environment we cocreate with teachers, parents, staff, and the entire school community shapes us, and we in turn are shaped by this environment.

How you think, what you experience day to day, can actually change the brain's physical structure. An often-cited study of London's black taxi cab drivers shows how. These cabbies are required to remember the over 25,000 London streets and hundreds of places of interest. The hippocampus is the region of the brain responsible for visual-spatial navigation and for consolidating short-term memory to long-term memory.

When examined for this study, researchers found that the hippocampus in the brains of the cabbies was larger and more developed, and the longer the cabbie drove a cab, the larger, more robust the hippocampus grew.

How Mindfulness Practice Changes the Brain

Studies show that mindfulness increases grey matter/cortical thickness in the anterior cingulate cortex (ACC), which is a structure located behind the brain's frontal lobe. It has been associated with such functions as self-regulatory processes, including the ability to monitor attention conflicts and allow for more cognitive flexibility.

Mindfulness enhances grey matter density in areas of the prefrontal lobe, which are primarily responsible for executive functioning such as planning, problem solving, and emotion regulation. Mindfulness studies have shown that the amygdala, known as our brain's "fight or flight" center and the seat of our fearful and anxious emotions, decreases in brain cell volume after mindfulness practice, addressing feelings of overwhelmingness.

Mindful Practice Pause

Try this brief 30-second mindful practice pause:

- Sit comfortably with spine straight but not rigid.
- Bring your attention to breathing.
- Aim and sustain your focus on your breathing.
- Notice when your attention is pulled away from this focus.
- Redirect your focus when you notice that your attention has strayed away from its focus.
- Stretch gently and notice how you feel.

Creativity: The Gold Standard of Mindful School Leadership

Creativity separates managers from leaders. Managers direct; leaders create—they make something new. The frontal lobe, the executive center of the brain, is associated with creative thinking. Mindfulness has been

(Continued)

(Continued)

shown to increase grey matter in this area of the brain and to reduce stress. Mindfulness helps school leaders slow down and disengage from daily overload and overwhelmingness.

Creativity requires slowing down.

We have a better chance of thinking creatively when we are not focused on multiple, tiny tasks, when we have space and time. The practice of stopping, pausing, noticing, and breathing allows school leaders to recenter, recharge, and regain mental, emotional, and spiritual centeredness in the moment. With regular mindfulness practice, school leaders are better able to be more creative in designing solutions to complex dilemmas. The intensity of school life has real consequences in burnout, chronic disease, and exhaustion.

The good news is that through mindfulness practices we can train ourselves to think more creatively without being swept away by a stream of mindless thinking. Mindfulness moments such as the practice pause here is one way to jump-start creativity, enhancing your leadership skills.

How Do Leaders Increase Their Own Self-Efficacy?

Self-efficacy doesn't just matter for students and teachers. Hattie's (2009) definition is "the confidence or strength of belief that we have in ourselves that we can make our learning happen." Without a high level of self-efficacy, leaders may never be able to lead effectively (Hannah, Avolio, Luthans, & Harms, 2008); this effective leadership is referred to as *leadership efficacy*. Hannah and colleagues suggest that leadership efficacy is "a specific form of efficacy associated with the level of confidence in the knowledge, skills, and abilities associated with leading others" (p. 670). They go on to define *leadership efficacy*: "Leaders' (followers') beliefs in their perceived capabilities to organize the positive psychological capabilities, motivation, means, collective resources, and courses of action required to attain effective, sustainable performance across their various leadership roles, demands, and contexts" (p. 671).

In looking at the Collaborative Leadership Framework one more time (see Figure 6.2), on which one of the following do you spend the most time? Why is that? What is it that you do that makes you collaborative or makes you feel you need to regulate everything?

Figure 6.2   Collaborative Leadership Framework

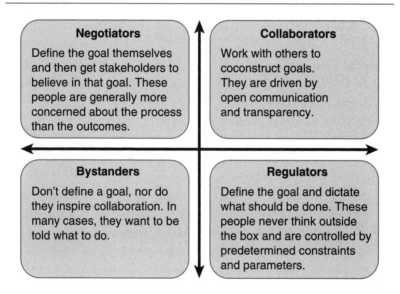

In Chapter 1, I introduced you to the Collaborative Leadership Growth Cycle. How can you use the growth cycle to help become more collaborative?

Bandura's work on self-efficacy was highlighted earlier as well, and I focused on four categories that help increase a level of self-efficacy. Those four categories are as important for leaders as they are for students and teachers. Bandura (1986) described those four areas as follows:

Personal performance accomplishments: A challenging activity brings out the strongest indicators for changing self-efficacy.

Vicarious experiences: McCormick, Tanguma, and López-Forment (2002) write, "By observing new skills and strategies in others, people enhance their task capabilities" (p. 43).

Positive feedback: Positive feedback helps to increase a person's level of self-efficacy.

Physiological condition: Social and emotional well-being matter because they contribute to a person's level of self-efficacy.

Personal Performance Accomplishments

If leaders are going to increase their own self-efficacy, they need to understand that sometimes the most difficult situations can help them learn. For example, earlier in the book I wrote that we had been through a school consolidation. The process that we went through as a school community—and the hardships that came with it—offered many learning lessons. Although many families, teachers, and staff were supportive and focused on helping the students of a one-classroom-per-grade-level school come to our own K–5 school, there were other parents and some board of education members who were not as positive. A parent created a hate blog that one board member contributed to anonymously, and other parents fought with one another on Facebook.

Over the three months before the new school year started, there were arguments at board meetings, name calling on social media, and letters written in the town paper that focused on how bad the consolidation would be for students, and they were all written by adults in the community. Over that time, I had to send out positive communication to combat all the negative communication. I wrote a letter to the board stating that we, as a school community, could make the consolidation work, and I had to have special open houses for new parents and PTA meetings that were enveloped by the consolidation.

Through that experience, and by consistently putting out positive messages during my leadership, I learned a great deal about adults and about myself. I certainly didn't do it alone because I was surrounded by a great staff and supportive families and students. In the end, after a year of trials and tribulations, we found ourselves with a personal professional accomplishment.

Vicarious Experiences

Vicarious experiences are very important for leaders if they are to increase their level of self-efficacy. If leaders pay attention, they are surrounded by vicarious experiences. Perhaps the experience comes from working with a fellow leadership colleague who excels at school safety or with a teacher colleague who has flawless teaching strategies that build student engagement. When *Collaborative Leadership: Six Influences That Matter Most* (2016a) was released, a group of K–12 leaders from Long Island, Westchester, and Rochester, New York; New Jersey; and Florida got together using the Voxer app on their phones. I was fortunate enough that they asked me to be a part of the group, and I joined. I learned through the experiences that each participant in the group Voxed about as they went from chapter to chapter in *Collaborative Leadership*.

In other experiences, I learned through watching leaders from other school districts during regional meetings. If leaders are open to learning when they walk into school or meetings, they will learn ways to increase their own self-efficacy. We need not get jealous or envious when another leader is doing something we didn't think of—we need to learn from them.

The Value of Positive Feedback

Positive feedback around social-emotional or academic goals is so vitally important to the growth of leaders, teachers, and students. As Bandura (1986) researched, positive feedback contributes to the self-efficacy of the person on the receiving end. This happens in a variety of ways. Leaders and teachers or teachers and students can coconstruct goals with one another around a specific learning intention. In addition to that specific learning intention, they set the success criteria, which means both parties understand how the goal is successful. Let's take that understanding and look at it through the leadership lens: The leader and teacher establish a goal and understand how it will be successful.

Perhaps the teacher and leader watch a video on Teaching Channel that helps illustrate what success looks like, or maybe a teacher visits a peer's classroom to observe the strategy in action. During this process, the leader provides feedback to the teacher to help her or him grow and gives feedback at the end that focuses on growth. That process leads to a stronger relationship between the teacher and leader and a stronger sense of self-efficacy for the teacher. Remember, this book focuses on school climate, and for that feedback process to be beneficial, the school climate needs to be one that is supportive.

The Tale of Two Principals

Tim Cooper—The school climate at Waterville High School fosters the type of feedback culture described earlier. Tim has open communication with his staff, with a focus on learning.

Trudy Cowen—The school climate at Eagle Elementary focuses more on compliance than on authentic learning. Trudy has not set the foundation for this type of feedback culture (it's never too late to turn around your leadership.)

Something to keep in mind when it comes to the complexities of feedback: Stone and Heen (2015) found that there are three triggers that receivers of feedback have when the feedback is given to them. The first of the feedback triggers is the Truth Trigger, in which the receiver is "upset about the substance or believe that it's off, unhelpful, or simply untrue." Then there is the Relationship Trigger, which is tripped by the particular person because "it's what we believe about the giver (no credibility!)." Finally, there is an Identity Trigger, which means that "it's hurting the identity we set for ourselves" (p. 16).

Leaders have the potential to receive feedback from staff, students, families, leadership colleagues, and central office administrators. It can be verbal, nonverbal, and written and can teach them a lot if they're paying attention.

Physiological Condition

Lastly, a leader's physiological condition is the last category in Bandura's recommended areas to improve self-efficacy, and that is sometimes the hardest to work on. We can look to *The 7 Habits of Highly Successful People*, where Covey (1989) offered up the following habits:

- Be proactive.
- Begin with the end in mind.
- Put first things first.
- Think win–win.
- Seek first to understand, then to be understood.
- Synergize.
- Sharpen the saw.

In addition to Covey's habits, leaders have to make sure they eat right, exercise, and get plenty of sleep, all of which are not easy to do. As a principal, I found it was easy to swipe candy from my secretary's desk or grab pizza from the lunchroom, and yes, I understand that school lunches can be the topic of another book. My sleeping pattern wasn't right either. I would wake up at 2 a.m. and be awake until about 3:30. It wasn't too long before the 2:00 to 3:30 sleepless time became a habit. The day's events or crisis situations left me thinking a lot and sleeping a little, and then I figured out one of the root causes. I was checking e-mail before I went to bed, and if there was even the slightest task that needed to be completed the following day, I found myself waking up in the middle of the night thinking about it. It literally took me a few years to realize that I needed to stop checking e-mail after 7 p.m., and quite honestly, I should not have checked it after I left the school building. Although 7 p.m. may be too early or too late for you, find a schedule that you can live with and try to stick with it.

Sharpen the saw by being with family and doing nonleadership activities. I was on the board of an AIDS organization and loved going to meetings and stuffing envelopes, serving food, or doing other rote activities just to give myself a brain break and focus on other, more critical issues that provided life perspective.

As a former distance runner, exercise has always been my saving grace. I loved pounding the pavement, and then after I injured myself so badly I could no longer run, I began biking, walking, and doing the elliptical machine or arc trainer. There is just no better escape than slapping on my headphones, grabbing my iPod, and listening to music and sweating at the same time. If leaders don't sharpen the saw, they don't increase their level of self-efficacy.

Stop. Collaborate and Listen!

- Make a list of everything you are responsible for doing—the good, the bad, and the indifferent.
- Go back through the list and highlight the things you like to do the most.
- Try your best every day or every week to spend most of your time in the highlighted section.
- Make an effort to spend time doing more of what you *want* to do and less of what you *have* to do.
- If your list is filled with things you don't like to do, then perhaps you need to make bigger changes in your job.

Additionally, Twitter and Facebook have offered invaluable experiences to me as a leader. Through Twitter, I have found a professional/personal learning network (PLN) that I learn from and stay connected to on a daily basis. The educators I have tweeted back and forth with have opened up my learning and helped me grow.

There are times when we are in a building-leadership role that we can become myopic. We believe that our issues are only the issues we have seen. The truth is that as I have grown in the role of consultant and author over the last three years, I have seen that our issues are often shared by most other leaders, and through conversations with them, we can grow and find our way out of them. We need to maintain this growth in order to effectively collaborate with staff, raise the self-efficacy of our stakeholders, and improve our school climates.

In the End

One of the most powerful pieces of research I have ever heard or read comes from Alessi.

> Alessi (1988) reviewed more than 5,000 children referred to school psychologists because they were failing at school. Not one located the problem as due to a poor instructional program, poor school practices, a poor teacher, or something to do with school. The problems were claimed, by the teachers, to be related to the home and located within the student. (Hattie, 2009, p. 52)

If leaders are truly going to meet, model, and motivate, then they have to do a bit of self-care in order to be effective. Without a high level of self-efficacy, leaders may never be able to lead effectively (Hannah et al., 2008). Bandura (1977, 1986, 1997) recommends that leaders increase their own self-efficacy through personal performance accomplishments, vicarious experiences, positive feedback, and physiological condition.

We know this is not easily done because when leaders are at the building level they are often caught between central office initiatives and teachers, students, and families.

Through creating PLNs and surrounding ourselves with people we can trust, we find the balance between being outspoken and being wrong. As Michael Fullan (2001) stated, we need to look past the policies and focus more inwardly on our mindsets as leaders. When we find that balance, we can build better school climates with our school community.

As you have read throughout the book, I believe leadership is hard because we have so many outside influences that are on our minds, such as school safety and the social-emotional well-being of our families who send their children to us. At the same time, we have new initiatives that need to take place and have to work on the collective efficacy of our staff, students, and families.

I believe that we need strong leaders now more than ever. We know that collaboration will help build the collective efficacy of the stakeholders within our schools, and we also know we have to prepare students to learn how to question the status quo, which takes a strong sense of self-efficacy. A positive and inclusive school climate can engage the unengaged and can maximize authentic learning experiences as opposed to compliant ones.

Thank you for taking the time to read this book. On page 178, you will find a leadership self-efficacy reflection activity. Please take the time to fill it out. I truly hope that you are able to put these ideas that you have learned from me or other voices in the book into action. We need more collaborative leaders. We need more leaders like you.

ACTION STEPS

- How will you focus on your own self-efficacy through feedback, vicarious experiences, positive feedback, and physiological condition?

- How will you make a bigger commitment to exercise, eat right, and get more sleep?
- Is it possible for you to practice some of Valerie Brown's mindfulness steps?
- How can you create your own PLN?

DISCUSSION QUESTIONS

- What does leadership self-efficacy mean to you?
- How do you feel about mindfulness?
- How will you move forward with district initiatives you don't necessarily agree with?
- How do you use social media for your professional/personal growth?

Leadership Self-Efficacy Scale

Instructions: Please indicate your personal opinion about each statement by circling the appropriate response at the right of each statement.

Key: 1 = Strongly agree, 2 = Moderately agree, 3 = Agree, 4 = Moderately disagree, 5 = Strongly disagree

1.	When I set important goals for myself, I achieve them.	1	2	3	4	5
2.	I learn important information about myself from a challenging situation.	1	2	3	4	5
3.	I feel like I am a better and much more prepared leader now than ever.	1	2	3	4	5
4.	I feel I have a growth mindset more than a fixed one (Dweck, 2007).	1	2	3	4	5
5.	I typically stand up and take the lead when a challenge arises.	1	2	3	4	5
6.	Accomplishing a task makes me feel good.	1	2	3	4	5
7.	I use evidence when I reflect on my practices because I want to understand why I'm successful or not.	1	2	3	4	5
8.	New learning inspires me.	1	2	3	4	5
9.	I may not be able to control the policies that come our way, but I do have control over my mindset when handling them.	1	2	3	4	5
10.	I am often successful.	1	2	3	4	5
11.	I do not practice the art of reflection because I do not have time for it.	1	2	3	4	5
12.	I avoid creating new professional goals because they require new learning.	1	2	3	4	5
13.	I avoid trying to learn new things when they look too difficult for me.	1	2	3	4	5
14.	I often feel insecure about my ability to lead.	1	2	3	4	5
15.	I give up easily on tasks that come my way.	1	2	3	4	5

Note: A lower overall score indicates a higher level of leadership efficacy.

Appendix

Collaborative Leadership Reflection Tool

The following are some reflective questions to answer. Answer them honestly in the comfort of a private setting. If you have a critical friend with whom to complete this, answer the questions and then discuss with her or him. This is not a judgment, but a reflective tool.

I'm not overly concerned with the goals of my staff as long as they don't get in the way of the task I need to complete in my office.	True	False
I don't know the goals of each staff member in my building.	True	False
I prefer to wait for staff, teachers, students, or families to contact me about an issue, even if I know about it first.	True	False
I prefer to sit back and listen to staff members during conversations to hear their line of thinking.	True	False
Meeting central-office needs is the most important aspect of my job.	True	False
I like to walk into a meeting with one idea and walk out with the same one.	True	False
I expect the notes from each PLC, grade level, or department meeting to make sure people are doing their jobs.	True	False

(Continued)

(Continued)

I set goals with each teacher before a formal observation so I know where I should aim my feedback.	True	False
I know I will find something for the teacher to improve on before I enter their classroom for an observation.	True	False
I check the lesson plans of all of my teachers on a consistent basis and hand them back with feedback they can read.	True	False
I discuss lesson plans with teachers on a consistent basis, and they give me insight into what students are learning so I can provide them with the best feedback possible.	True	False
I need to get the answers to my questions on a regular basis.	True	False
I listen to other people's concerns fully before I provide my insight.	True	False
I try my best to say *our* faculty and *our* school instead of *my* faculty and *my* school.	True	False
I do not have to have all of the answers before I walk into the meeting because I know the collective power of the staff will come up with the best solution to our problem.	True	False
I often have meetings after a meeting because I want to further explain my goal.	True	False
I steer the conversation with staff toward my idea, but in the end, I want them to think it's actually their idea so they're on board.	True	False
I need to have all of the answers before I go into an individual or group meeting.	True	False
I don't really like to question initiatives coming from central office.	True	False
I like to build consensus.	True	False

I am OK with faculty asking me any question in a faculty meeting. I prefer to discuss the elephant in the room and come out with a better understanding of the mindset of staff.	True	False
I don't mind respectful confrontation, as long as it leads to a better place for both of us.	True	False
It is important for me to foster opportunities for all staff members to share their voices.	True	False
I make sure that those teachers who dominate meetings understand that everyone has the right to talk.	True	False

Leadership Style: _____

Faculty Meeting Exit Ticket

What follows is an example of an exit ticket that leaders can use after their faculty meetings. Simply provide it to staff at the end of the meeting, have them fill it out, and place it on a table on the way out of the meeting. Additionally, this could be used as part of an online survey form.

1. What was one thing you learned at the meeting?

    _____

    _____

    _____

2. How will you use it?

    _____

    _____

    _____

3. What were you hoping to learn?

    _____

    _____

    _____

4. What would you like us to do differently next time?

    _____

    _____

    _____

Teacher Efficacy Scale (Short Form)*

Hoy and Woolfolk (1993) offer a more in-depth efficacy scale for teachers to fill out. With their permission, here are some of the questions from their scale, along with the website to visit for further information if leaders and teachers want to explore teacher efficacy further.

Instructions: Please indicate your personal opinion about each statement by circling the appropriate response to the right of each statement.

Key: 1 = Strongly agree, 2 = Moderately agree, 3 = Agree slightly more than disagree, 4 = Disagree slightly more than agree, 5 = Moderately disagree, 6 = Strongly disagree

The amount a student can learn is primarily related to family background.	1	2	3	4	5	6
If students aren't disciplined at home, they aren't likely to accept any discipline.	1	2	3	4	5	6
When I really try, I can get through to most difficult students.	1	2	3	4	5	6
A teacher is very limited in what he or she can achieve because a student's home environment is a large influence on his or her achievement.	1	2	3	4	5	6
If parents would do more for their children, I could do more.	1	2	3	4	5	6

Source: Hoy, W. K., & Woolfolk, A. E. (1993). Teachers' sense of efficacy and the organizational health of schools. *The Elementary School Journal 93*, 356–372.

*For more information on this scale, visit http://u.osu.edu/hoy.17/research/instruments and http://www.waynekhoy.com/collective_efficacy.html

Collective Teacher Efficacy Scale

This is a collective teacher efficacy scale by Megan Tschannen-Moran, College of William and Mary. The scoring directions follow. In order to find the full collective teacher efficacy scale, please visit http://wmpeople.wm.edu/site/page/mxtsch/researchtools.

	None at All		Very Little		Some Degree		Quite a Bit		A Great Deal
1. How much can teachers in your school do to produce meaningful student learning?	1	2	3	4	5	6	7	8	9
2. How much can your school do to get students to believe they can do well in schoolwork?	1	2	3	4	5	6	7	8	9
3. To what extent can teachers in your school make expectations clear about appropriate student behavior?	1	2	3	4	5	6	7	8	9
4. To what extent can school personnel in your school establish rules and procedures that facilitate learning?	1	2	3	4	5	6	7	8	9

	None at All		Very Little		Some Degree		Quite a Bit		A Great Deal
5. How much can teachers in your school do to help students master complex content?	1	2	3	4	5	6	7	8	9
6. How much can teachers in your school do to promote deep understanding of academic concepts?	1	2	3	4	5	6	7	8	9
7. How well can teachers in your school respond to defiant students?	1	2	3	4	5	6	7	8	9
8. How much can school personnel in your school do to control disruptive behavior?	1	2	3	4	5	6	7	8	9
9. How much can teachers in your school do to help students think critically?	1	2	3	4	5	6	7	8	9
10. How well can adults in your school get students to follow school rules?	1	2	3	4	5	6	7	8	9
11. How much can your school do to foster student creativity?	1	2	3	4	5	6	7	8	9

(Continued)

(Continued)

	None at All	Very Little	Some Degree	Quite a Bit	A Great Deal
12. How much can your school do to help students feel safe while they are at school?	1 2	3 4	5 6	7 8	9

Developer: Megan Tschannen-Moran, College of William and Mary. Tschannen-Moran, M., & Barr, M. (2004). Fostering Student Learning: The Relationship of Collective Teacher Efficacy and Student Achievement. *Leadership and Policy in Schools,* 3(3), 189–209.

Directions for Scoring the Collective Teacher Efficacy Scale

Construct Validity

Construct validity of the Collective Teacher Efficacy Scale was established through factor analysis. Two strong factors emerge that were moderately correlated. When a second order factor analysis was conducted, the two factors formed a single factor.

Subscale Scores

An overall collective teacher efficacy score can be computed by taking a mean of all 12 items. To determine the *Collective Efficacy in Instructional Strategies* and the *Collective Efficacy in Student Discipline* subscale scores, compute a mean score of the items that relate to each factor.

Instructional Strategies

1. How much can teachers in your school do to produce meaningful student learning?

2. How much can your school do to get students to believe they can do well in schoolwork?

3. How much can teachers in your school do to help students master complex content?

4. How much can teachers in your school do to promote deep understanding of academic concepts?

5. How much can teachers in your school do to help students think critically?

6. How much can your school do to foster student creativity?

Student Discipline

7. To what extent can teachers in your school make expectations clear about appropriate student behavior?

8. To what extent can school personnel in your school establish rules and procedures that facilitate learning?

9. How well can teachers in your school respond to defiant students?

10. How much can school personnel in your school do to control disruptive behavior?

11. How well can adults in your school get students to follow school rules?

12. How much can your school do to help students feel safe while they are at school?

Leadership Self-Efficacy Scale

Instructions: Please indicate your personal opinion about each statement by circling the appropriate response at the right of each statement.

Key: 1 = Strongly agree, 2 = Moderately agree, 3 = Agree, 4 = Moderately disagree, 5 = Strongly disagree

1. When I set important goals for myself, I achieve them.	1	2	3	4	5
2. I learn important information about myself from a challenging situation.	1	2	3	4	5
3. I feel like I am a better and much more prepared leader now than ever.	1	2	3	4	5
4. I feel I have a growth mindset more than a fixed one (Dweck, 2007).	1	2	3	4	5
5. I typically stand up and take the lead when a challenge arises.	1	2	3	4	5
6. Accomplishing a task makes me feel good.	1	2	3	4	5
7. I use evidence when I reflect on my practices because I want to understand why I'm successful or not.	1	2	3	4	5
8. New learning inspires me.	1	2	3	4	5
9. I may not be able to control the policies that come our way, but I do have control over my mindset when handling them.	1	2	3	4	5
10. I am often successful.	1	2	3	4	5
11. I do not practice the art of reflection because I do not have time for it.	1	2	3	4	5

12.	I avoid creating new professional goals because they require new learning.	1	2	3	4	5
13.	I avoid trying to learn new things when they look too difficult for me.	1	2	3	4	5
14.	I often feel insecure about my ability to lead.	1	2	3	4	5
15.	I give up easily on tasks that come my way.	1	2	3	4	5

Note: A lower overall score indicates a higher level of leadership efficacy.

References

Alessi, G. (1988). Diagnosis diagnosed: A systemic reaction. *Professional School Psychology, 3*, 145–151.

Angelle, P. S., & DeHart, C. A. (2011). Teacher perceptions of teacher leadership: Examining differences by experience, degree, and position. *NASSP Bulletin, 95*(2), 141–160.

Ashton, P., Webb, R., & Doda, N. (1982). A study of teacher's sense of efficacy. (Final report to the National Institute of Education, Volume II [Appendices]). Gainesville, FL: Florida University.

Ashton, P. T., & Webb, R. B. (1986). *Making a difference: Teachers' sense of efficacy and student achievement.* New York, NY: Longman.

Bandura, A. (1977). Self-efficacy: Toward a unifying theory of behavioral change. *Psychological Review, 84*(2), 191–215.

Bandura, A. (1986). *Social foundations of thought and action.* Englewood Cliffs, NJ: Prentice-Hall.

Bandura, A. (1994). Self-efficacy. In V. S. Ramachaudran (Ed.), *Encyclopedia of human behavior* (Vol. 4, pp. 71–81). New York, NY: Academic Press.

Bandura, A. (1997). *Self-efficacy: The exercise of control.* New York, NY: W. H. Freeman.

Bartik, T. J. (2013, January 31). *Family income, student achievement, and educational costs.* Presented at the Kalamazoo Public Schools Board of Education meeting, Kalamazoo, MI.

Berkowitz, R., Moore, H., Avi Astor, R., & Benbenishty, R. (2016). A research synthesis of the associations between socioeconomic background, inequality, school climate, and academic achievement. *Review of Educational Research, 87*(2), 425–469. Retrieved from https://doi.org/10.3102/0034654316669821

Bishop, R. (2010). Effective teaching for indigenous and minoritized students: International conference on learner diversity—2010. *Procedia Social and Behavioral Sciences, 7*(C), 57–62.

Bishop, R., & Berryman, M. (2006). *Culture speaks: Cultural relationships and classroom learning.* Wellington, New Zealand: Huia.

Bishop, R., & Berryman, M. (2009). *The Te Kotahitanga effective teaching profile: Set 2, 2009—Edited extracts.* Christchurch, New Zealand: Linwood College. Retrieved from http://www.linwoodcollege.school.nz/sites/default/files/TeKotahitangaETPculturally-responsive%20teaching.pdf

Blad, E. (2016, August 1). Social-emotional learning: States collaborate to craft standards, policies [Blog post]. *Education Week.* Retrieved from http://blogs.edweek.org/edweek/rulesfor engagement/2016/08/social-emotional_learning_states_colla borate_to_craft_standards_policies.html

Brown, V. (2015, August 16). Leading from within: Mindfulness practices for school leaders [Blog post]. *Education Week.* Retrieved from http://blogs.edweek.org/edweek/finding_common_ground/2015/08/leading_from_within_mindfulness_practices_for_school_leaders.html

Bruce, C., & Flynn, T. (2013). Assessing the effects of collaborative professional learning: Efficacy shifts in a three-year mathematics study. *Alberta Journal of Educational Research, 58*(4), 691–709.

Burris, C. C. (2014). *On the same track: How schools can join the twenty-first century struggle against resegregation.* Boston, MA: Beacon Press.

Campbell, C., Osmond-Johnson, P., Faubert, B., Zeichner, K., & Hobbs-Johnson, A. (2016). *The state of educators' professional learning in Canada.* Oxford, OH: Learning Forward.

Clarke, S. (2009). Using curriculum-based measurement to improve achievement. *Principal.* Reston, VA: National Association of Elementary School Principals.

Clinton, J., Hattie, J., & Dixon, R. (2007). *Evaluation of the Flaxmere Project: When families learn the language of school.* University of Auckland: Report for the Ministry of Education.

Coe, R. (2002). *It's the effect size, stupid: What effect size is and why it's important.* Durham, NC: School of Education, University of Durham.

Collaborative for Academic, Social, and Emotional Learning. (2017). *What is SEL?* Retrieved from http://www.casel.org/faqs/

Constantino, S. M. (2016). *Engage every family: Five simple principles.* Thousand Oaks, CA: Corwin.

Covey, S. (1989). *The 7 Habits of Highly Successful People.* New York, NY: Simon and Schuster.

Darling-Hammond, L., Austin K., Cheung, M., & Martin, D. (2003). *Thinking about thinking: Metacognition.* Stanford, CA: Stanford University.

DeWitt, P. (2011, November 1). Student-led conferences [Blog post]. *Education Week.* Retrieved from http://blogs.edweek.org/edweek/finding_common_ground/2011/11/student-led_conferences.html

DeWitt, P. (2012). *Dignity for all: Safeguarding LGBT students.* Thousand Oaks, CA: Corwin.

DeWitt, P. (2014). *Flipping leadership doesn't mean reinventing the wheel.* Thousand Oaks, CA: Corwin.

DeWitt, P. (2016a). *Collaborative leadership: Six influences that matter most.* Thousand Oaks, CA: Corwin.

DeWitt, P. (2016b, June 15). Is your parent engagement authentic or compliant? [Blog post]. *Education Week.*

DeWitt, P. (2016c, August 21). What are the best strategies for surface to deep level learning? [Blog post]. *Education Week.*

DeWitt, P. (2016d, November 15). School climate: Avoiding tough conversations limits our learning [Blog post]. *Education Week.* Retrieved from http://blogs.edweek.org/edweek/finding_common_ground/2016/11/school_climate_why_avoiding_tough_conversations_limits_our_learning.html

DeWitt, P., & Donohoo, J. (2016, November 20). Why collaborative inquiry? Professional learning that makes a difference [Blog post]. *Education Week.* Retrieved from http://blogs.edweek.org/edweek/finding_common_ground/2016/11/why_collaborative_inquiry_professional_learning_that_makes_a_difference.html

DeWitt, P., & Slade, S. (2014). *School climate change: How do I build a positive environment for learning?* Alexandria, VA: Association for Supervision and Curriculum Development.

Donohoo, J. (2016). *Collective efficacy: How educators' beliefs impact student learning.* Thousand Oaks, CA: Corwin.

Donohoo, J., & Velasco, M. (2016). *The transformative power of collaborative inquiry: Realizing change in schools and classrooms.* Thousand Oaks, CA: Corwin.

Durlak, J. A., Weissberg, R. P., Dymnicki, A. B., Taylor, R. D., & Schellinger, K. B. (2011). The impact of enhancing students' social and emotional learning: A meta-analysis of school-based universal interventions. *Child Development, 82*(1), 405–432.

Dweck, C. S. (2007). *Mindset: The new psychology of success.* New York, NY: Ballantine Books.

Eells, R. (2011). *Meta-analysis of the relationship between collective teacher efficacy and student achievement.* Doctoral dissertation. Loyola University.

Fisher, D., Frey, N., & Hattie, J. (2016). *Visible learning for literacy: Implementing the practices that work best to accelerate student learning.* Thousand Oaks, CA: Corwin.

Fraser, B. J. (1994). Research on classroom and school climate. In D. Gabel (Ed.), *Handbook of research on science teaching and learning* (pp. 493–541). New York, NY: Macmillan.

Fuchs, L. S., Deno, S. L., & Mirkin, P. K. (1984). The effects of frequent curriculum-based measurement and evaluation on pedagogy, student achievement, and student awareness of learning. *American Educational Research Journal, 21*(2), 449–460.

Fullan, M. (2001). *Leading in a culture of change.* San Francisco, CA: Jossey-Bass

Fullan, M., & Hargreaves, A. (2016). *Call to action: Bringing the profession back in.* Oxford, OH: Learning Forward. Retrieved from https://learningforward.org/docs/default-source/pdf/bringing-the-profession-back-in.pdf

Gable, S., Krull, J. L., & Chang, Y. (2012). Boys' and girls' weight status and math performance from kindergarten entry through fifth grade: A mediated analysis. *Child Development, 83*(5), 1822–1839.

Gallup. (2016). *Gallup Student Poll 2015 results.* Retrieved from http://www.gallup.com/services/189926/student-poll-2015-results.aspx

Gargani, J., & Strong, M. (2014, November/December). Can we identify a successful teacher better, faster, and cheaper? Evidence for innovating teacher observation systems. *Journal of Teacher Education, 65*(5), 389–401.

Goddard, R., Hoy, W., & Woolfolk Hoy, A. (2004). Collective efficacy beliefs: Theoretical developments, empirical evidence, and future directions. *American Educational Research Association, 33*(3), 3–13.

Goddard, R. D., Hoy, W. K., & Woolfolk Hoy, A. (2000). Collective teacher efficacy: Its meaning, measure, and impact on student achievement. *American Educational Research Journal, 37*(2), 479–507.

Hallinger, P., & Heck, R. H. (1996). Reassessing the principal's role in school effectiveness: A review of empirical research, 1980–1995. *Educational Administration Quarterly, 32*(1), 5–44.

Hallinger, P., & Heck, R. (2010). Leadership for learning: Does collaborative leadership make a difference in school improvement? *Educational Management Administration & Leadership, 38*(6), 654–678.

Halpin, A. W., & Croft, D. B. (1963). *The organizational climate of schools.* Chicago, IL: Midwest Administration Center of the University of Chicago.

Hannah, S. T., Avolio, B., Luthans, F., & Harms, P. D. (2008). Leadership efficacy: Review and future directions. *Management Department Faculty Publications,* Paper 5.

Hargreaves, A., & Fullan, M. (2012). *Professional capital: Transforming teaching in every school.* New York, NY: Teachers College Press.

Harper, S. R. (2012, Fall). Race without racism: How higher education researchers minimize racist institutional norms. *The Review of Higher Education, 36*(1), Supplement, pp. 9–29.

Harwell, M., & LeBeau, B. (2010, March 10). Student eligibility for a free lunch as an SES measure in education research. *Educational Researcher, 39,* 120–131.

Hattie, J. (2009). *Visible learning: A synthesis of over 800 meta-analyses relating to achievement.* London, England: Routledge.

Hattie, J. (2012a). *Visible learning for teachers: Maximizing impact on learning.* London, England: Routledge.

Hattie, J. (2012b, September). Know thy impact: Educational leadership. *Feedback for Learning, 70*(1), 18–23.

Hattie, J. (2015a). Hattie ranking: 195 influences and effect sizes related to student achievement. Retrieved from https://visible-learning.org/hattie-ranking-influences-effect-sizes-learning-achievement/

Hattie, J. (2015b). *Know thy impact: Visible learning in theory and practice.* London, England: Routledge.

Hattie, J. (2015c). *The power of collaborative expertise.* London, England: Pearson.

Hattie, J. (2015d). *What doesn't work in education: Politics of distraction.* London, England: Pearson.

Hattie, J. (2016, November). Personal communication.

Hattie, J., & Donoghue, G. (2016). Learning strategies: A synthesis and conceptual model. *npj Science of Learning, 1.* Retrieved from https://www.nature.com/articles/npjscilearn201613

Headlee, C. (2016, February 16). *Ten ways to have a better conversation* [TED talk]. Retrieved from https://www.ted.com/talks/celeste_headlee_10_ways_to_have_a_better_conversation

Henderson, A. T., & Mapp, K. L. (2002). *A new wave of evidence: The impact of school, family, and community connections on student achievement*. Austin, TX: National Center for Family and Community Connections With Schools.

Hoy, W. K., & Woolfolk, A. E. (1993). Teachers' sense of efficacy and the organizational health of schools. *The Elementary School Journal, 93,* 356–372.

Huggins, K. S., Klar, H. W., Hammonds, H., & Buskey, F. C. (2016). Supporting leadership development: An examination of high school principals' efforts to develop leaders' personal capacities. *Journal of Research on Leadership Education, 11*(2), 200–221.

Hughes, W., & Pickeral, T. (2013). *School climate and shared leadership.* New York, NY: National School Climate Center.

Johnson, B., & McClure, R. (2004). Validity and reliability of a shortened, revised version of the constructivist learning environment survey (CLES). *Learning Environments Research, 7,* 65.

Jones, B. D. (2007). The unintended outcomes of high-stakes testing. *Journal of Applied School Psychology, 23*(2).

Katz, S., & Dack, L. A. (2013). *Intentional interruption: Breaking down learning barriers to transform professional practice.* Thousand Oaks, CA: Corwin.

Killian, S. (2015). An objective critique of Hattie's visible learning research. *Australian Society for Evidence-Based Teaching,* 1–5. Retrieved from http://www.evidencebasedteaching.org.au/wp-content/uploads/2015/07/An-Objective-Critique-of-Hatties-Visible-Learning-Research.pdf

Knight, J. (2007). *Instructional coaching: A partnership approach to improving instruction.* Thousand Oaks, CA: Corwin.

Knight, J. (2014). *Focus on teaching: Using video for high-impact instruction.* Thousand Oaks, CA: Corwin.

Kosciw, J. G., Greytak, E. A., Palmer, N. A., & Boesen, M. J. (2014). *The 2013 National School Climate Survey: The experiences of lesbian, gay, bisexual and transgender youth in our nation's schools.* New York, NY: GLSEN. Retrieved from https://www.glsen.org/sites/default/files/2013%20National%20School%20Climate%20Survey%20Full%20Report_0.pdf

Kuhn, D. (2015, January/February). Thinking together and alone. *Educational Research, 44*, 146–153.

Lai, E., & Cheung, D. (2015, September). Enacting teacher leadership: The role of teachers in bringing about change. *Educational Management Administration Leadership, 43*(5), 673–692.

Leithwood, K., Jantzi, D., Earl, L., Watson, N., Levin, B., & Fullan, M. (2004). Strategic leadership for large-scale reform: The case of England's national literacy and numeracy strategy. *School Leadership & Management, 24*(1), 57–79.

Leithwood, K., & Mascall, B. (2008, October). Collective leadership effects on student achievement. *Educational Administration Quarterly, 44*(4), 529–561.

Lopez, S. J., & Sidhu, P. (2013, August 1). In U.S., newer teachers most likely to be engaged at work. Gallup. Retrieved from http://www.gallup.com/poll/163745/newer-teachers-likely-engaged-work.aspx

Margolis, H., & McCabe, P. P. (2003). Self-efficacy: A key to improving the motivation of struggling learners. *Preventing School Failure: Alternative Education for Children and Youth, 47*(4).

McCormick, M. J., Tangum, J., & López-Forment, A. S. (2002, Winter). Extending self-efficacy theory to leadership: A review and empirical test. *Journal of Leadership Education, 1*(2), 34–49.

National School Climate Center. (n.d.). *School climate.* Retrieved from http://www.schoolclimate.org/climate/

Olsen, K., & Brown, V. (2012, June 29). Developing mindfulness in school leaders. *Education Week.*

Partnership for 21st Century Learning. (2016, January). *Framework for 21st century learning.* Retrieved from http://www.p21.org/our-work/p21-framework

Pickeral, T. (2016, November 21). Ten recommendations for implementing school climate reform in schools [Blog post]. Retrieved from http://terrypickeral.com/index.php/2016/11/20/10-recommendations-for-implementing-school-climate-reform-in-schools/

Quaglia, R., & Lande, L. (2015). *Teacher voice report: Quaglia Institute for student aspirations and teacher voice and aspirations.* International Center, in partnership and with support from Corwin and Southern New Hampshire University.

Quaglia, R., & Lande, L. (2017). *Teacher voice: Amplifying success.* Thousand Oaks, CA: Corwin.

Reeves, D. (2002). *The daily disciplines of leadership: How to improve student achievement, staff motivation, and personal organization.* San Francisco, CA: Jossey-Bass.

Robinson, V. (2011). *Student-centered leadership.* San Francisco, CA: Jossey-Bass.

Rowe, E. W., Sangwon, K., Baker, J. A., Kamphaus, R. W., & Horne, A. W. (2010). Student personal perception of classroom climate: Exploratory and confirmatory factor analyses. *Educational and Psychological Measurement, 70*(5), 858–879.

Schleicher, A. (2008). *Improving school leadership policy and practice in OECD countries.* Paris, France: Organisation for Economic and Co-Operational Development.

Shernoff, D. J., Ruzek, E. A., & Sinha, S. (2016). The influence of the high school classroom environment on learning as mediated by student engagement. *School Psychology International,* 1–18.

Singh, G. K., Siahpush, M., Hiatt, R. A., & Timsina, L. R. (2011). Dramatic increases in obesity and overweight prevalence and body mass index among ethnic-immigrant and social class groups in the United States, 1976–2008. *Journal of Community Health, 36*(1), 94–110. Retrieved from http://doi.org/10.1007/s10900-010-9287-9

Singh, G. K., Siahpush, M., & Kogan, M. D. (2010). Rising social inequalities in U.S. childhood obesity, 2003–2007. *Annals of Epidemiology, 20*(1), 40–52.

Stone, D., & Heen, S. (2015). *Thanks for the feedback: The science and art of receiving feedback well.* New York, NY: Penguin Books.

Timperley, H., Wilson, A., Barrar, H., & Fung, I. (2007). *Teacher professional learning and development: Best evidence synthesis iteration.* Wellington, New Zealand: Ministry of Education.

Tschannen-Moran, M., & Barr, M. (2004). Fostering student learning: The relationship of collective teacher efficacy and student achievement. *Leadership and Policy in Schools, 3*(3), 189–209.

Turner, C. (2014, April). U.S. tests teens lot, but worldwide, exam stakes are higher. *All Things Considered.* National Public Radio.

United States Government Accountability Office. (2010, November). *K–12 education: Many challenges arise in educating students who change schools frequently.*

Voelkel, R. Jr. (2011). *A case study of the relationship between collective efficacy and professional learning communities.* Unpublished doctoral dissertation. University of California, San Diego, California State University, San Marcos.

Wandall, J. (2011, May). National tests in Denmark: CAT as a pedagogic tool. *Journal of Applied Testing Technology, 12.*

Weiss, H. B., Lopez, M. E., & Rosenberg, H. (2010, December). Harvard family research project: Beyond random acts—Family, school, and community engagement as an integral part of education reform. *National Policy Forum for Family, School, & Community Engagement.*

Wells, N. M., & Evans, G. W. (2003, May). Nearby nature: A buffer of life stress among rural children. *Environment and Behavior, 35*(3), 311–330.

West, M. (2012, August 16). *Is retaining students in the early grades self-defeating?* Washington, DC: Brookings Institution.

World Health Organization. (2001a, October 1). The World Health Report 2001—*Mental health: New understanding, new hope* [Press release]. Retrieved from http://www.who.int/whr/2001/en/

World Health Organization. (2001b, October 4). *Mental disorders affect one in four people: Treatment available but not being used* [Press release]. Retrieved from http://www.who.int/whr/2001/media_centre/press_release/en/

Index

Notes

Notes

Notes

Notes

CORWIN LEADERSHIP

Leadership that Makes an Impact

Charlotte Danielson
Harness the power of informal professional conversation and invite teachers to boost achievement.

Liz Wiseman, Lois Allen, & Elise Foster
Use leadership to bring out the best in others—liberating staff to excel and doubling your team's effectiveness.

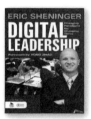

Eric Sheninger
Use digital resources to create a new school culture, increase engagement, and facilitate real-time PD.

Russell J. Quaglia, Michael J. Corso, & Lisa L. Lande
Listen to your school's voice to see how you can increase engagement, involvement, and academic motivation.

Michael Fullan, Joanne Quinn, & Joanne McEachen
Learn the right drivers to mobilize complex, coherent, whole-system change and transform learning for all students.

CORWIN LEADERSHIP

A SAGE Publishing Company

CORWIN HAS ONE MISSION: to enhance education through intentional professional learning.

We build long-term relationships with our authors, educators, clients, and associations who partner with us to develop and continuously improve the best evidence-based practices that establish and support lifelong learning.

ONTARIO
PRINCIPALS'
COUNCIL
Exemplary Leadership in Public Education

The Ontario Principals' Council (OPC) is a voluntary association for principals and vice-principals in Ontario's public school system. We believe that exemplary leadership results in outstanding schools and improved student achievement. To this end, we foster quality leadership through world-class professional services and supports. We are committed to **"quality leadership—our principal product."**

Solutions you want. Experts you trust. Results you need.